# All the King's Children

## THE HUMAN LEGACY OF ALEX SANDERS

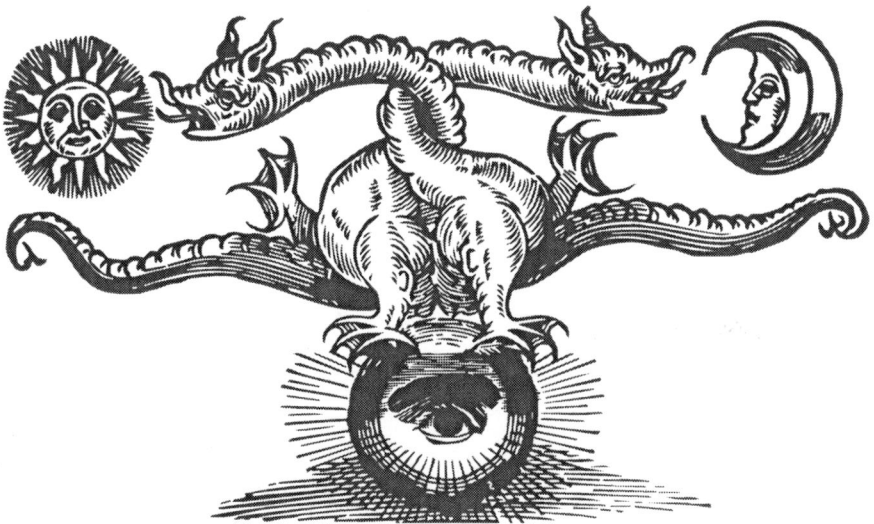

# JIMAHL DI FIOSA

This book is dedicated to Maxine Sanders.
As she told me recently over a good cup of Yorkshire tea,
"Power finds its way."

**Alex Sanders**
**King of the Witches**

*"What is a man anyhow? What am I? And what are you?*
*All I mark as my own you shall offset it with your own.*
*Else it were time lost listening to me."*

Walt Whitman

**All the King's Children**
The Human Legacy of Alex Sanders
By Jimahl diFiosa

2010 LOGIOS©
2015 LOGIOS©
Published by LOGIOS©
www.logiosprojects.com

LOGIOS

Printed in the United States of America
ISBN: 9781320444613

Second Edition

Cover art and book design by Karagan
Edited by Joseph D. Carriker, Jr.
Photograph of Alex Sanders courtesy of
John Hooper - Hoopix® /The Museum of Witchcraft UK

# Acknowledgements

Thank you to all of the wonderful men and women who shared their stories with me so freely.

Thank you for your courage, your honesty, your trust, and your patience in dealing with all of the emails, deadlines and long distance phone calls. I hope I have told your story well. Thanks to Karagan for enduring the madness of the creative process with me, and for his amazing cover art and book design. Thanks to Joseph for editing the book so beautifully. And to Beck who read the first draft in its roughest form and provided such brilliat feedback. Without all of you, this book would still be rattling around in my head.

I'm glad we set it free.

# Contents

# Preface

*C*hances are if you bought this book you fall into one of three categories. You are an initiate of the Craft, possibly even Alexandrian. You have an interest, academic or otherwise, in the subject of witchcraft today and want to learn more.Or like everyone else – you are just trying to find the road that leads you home at the end of the day. Ultimately this book is about a spiritual quest. Not mine and not those of the wonderful people who will share their stories with you, but your own.

Whether or not we realize it, we are all seekers. It is our nature to leave no stone unturned, to look behind every tree in the forest, and to want to know what's just around the next bend.

Seekers are never satisfied with hearing "that's the way it always was" or "leave it alone." We realize that there is value to asking questions and expecting answers. To push a little harder and go a little farther, even if it means making our way in the world one measured step at a time.

This book will serve that purpose well because it is a collection of stories about people like you. People who follow their heart and who are not afraid to dream impossible dreams. People who know that there is room in the universe for everyone and that each of us is entitled to our unique vision.

By definition, this book is about Alexandrian initiates – the children of a king. The king, of course, being Alex Sanders. There has been a lot of controversy about the king business. To clarify, "king" in this context was never meant to imply that Alex ruled the universe. It was not a title he gave himself, but an honorary title given to him by his own witches. He was definitely not the king of all witches. Frankly, who would want to be?

Such silly pronouncements are best left to braggarts and fools and Alex was neither. Alex received the title with a humble heart. He was a reluctant king.

Alex presented a new version of the Craft to the world that was colorful, powerful and deeply rooted in magic. It is not a shallow pool in which to swim and still today is one of the most challenging Wiccan disciplines. Those who embrace Alex's unique vision and follow in his footsteps are doubly blessed. They have inherited a system of magic that works (and in my opinion is second to none). And they have the benefit of shared experience because they are connected not only to Alex but to all those who came before, and to all who will come after.

The stories shared in this book represent just a small part of the vast human legacy of Alex Sanders. The stories are shared candidly. The tellers hold nothing back. Their lives reflect the depth and beauty of Alexandrian Craft.

How many Alexandrian initiates are there in the world today? I don't think it is possible to get an accurate count. Personally, I have the honor of counting hundreds as my friends. These initiates span the globe – throughout the United Kingdom and all of Western Europe to Australia, New Zealand and the United States and Canada.

Much has been written about Alex Sanders but much more has been left unsaid about the men and women whose lives were changed forever by knowing this remarkable man. What makes these stories unique is not that the tellers of the stories are Alexandrian witches, or even that they are witches at all, but that each of the stories speak to the resolute nature of the human condition. To that mysterious "x factor" that moves us forward when the rational mind says stop. To that which moves us beyond the world of form to the world of spirit where what matters most is not breath, but heart.

# Home Before Dark

Lyn Nitz-Mercaeant
Third Degree High Priestess
United States of America

*The little girl from the fishing camp had gone far into the woods –
farther than any other white child had gone. She stops running for a second and
looks for the path beneath her feet. It is getting dark and the colors of the forest
meld together into a deep dark brown that rolls over her like a blanket. Her heart
pounds in her tiny chest and she feels a sudden urge to cry. "I'm lost", she thinks and
then puts a lid on that fear as if she were shutting a box. She knows that crying
won't help and the other children who live in the woods will laugh at her. She tries
to remember what she has been taught about the forest, what to do when you stay
out far too late and the day comes crashing in around you. There is a sound of
an animal moving in the brush behind her. "There are coyotes in the woods," she
thinks, and then with another sudden rush of fear, "Bears! Coyotes and bears eat
children." The thought is out there before she can pull it back. And then she can't
help it. She starts running again, racing against the sliding light of day to find
her way home...*

I was born in Chicago, Illinois, USA. My parents, who are both
now on the other side of the Veil, were loving and caring individuals who
allowed me space to be and explore who I was as a child and adolescent.
My mom was always there, she was strict but always kind. My father and
I used to escape and do stuff together, such as rock hounding and fishing.
He liked the outdoors. I found out after he passed over that he was an active
member of the Edgar Cayce Society.

I am an only child. However, when I was twenty-two I found out
that I was adopted when I was born. My birth parents were of Scot/Irish
(Mom) and French (Dad) descent. The adoption came as a surprise to me.
My birth mother had extreme medical issues and my adoptive parents kept
it from me because they didn't want to lose me. Once I found out the details
it made it less traumatic. I have a piece of tartan from my birth mom that
has enabled me to trace my original family back to a Scottish clan.

My parents were American Synod Lutheran. However, the only
time they went to church was once a month on Communion Sunday. So my
parents weren't particularly religious, but there was religion.

Every summer from the ages of seven to fourteen, I went to stay
with my Aunt who owned a fishing resort on a lake in Northern Minnesota.
Those summers had a big impact on me. I got a very up close and personal
look at nature by being exposed to it for months at a time. My days were
spent running with the American Indian (Ojibwe) kids as they tried hard
to lose the little white girl in the forest. I gained an appreciation for nature
that one only experiences by being immersed in it. That time of my life was

so beautiful.

The American Indian children would basically make fun of the little white girl. They would run ahead of me and leave me running after them. I learned a lot during those summers. I foraged for berries and learned which plants and roots were good to eat. Because I developed these wildcrafting skills in early years, I came into the Craft with a deep reverence for nature. The Ojibwe children taught me to revere every living thing and to take the time to experience the natural world. I remember lying under the stars with them and watching the Northern Lights, experiencing it through their eyes. "Look at those colors. This is how we view this." In the summer of my fourteenth year, the Ojibwe Tribe gave me a coming of age ceremony. My forest friends made me a beaded headband with symbols of all of the things I learned over those seven summers.

As an adult and a witch, I now understand that seeing nature in such an intimate way makes it impossible to be passive about it. I now have a firsthand appreciation for nature.

It was late in my fourteenth year that I had my first exposure to the occult. I had a girlfriend who owned a deck of Tarot cards and I asked her to teach me to read them. She gave me the cards to look at and I was amazed. She explained that each card tells a story. She agreed to teach me on one condition – that I don't tell my mother. She said it was important that we keep this a secret. Of course I agreed and she started me on my first baby steps into learning the art of Tarot. After a while I became very good at it.

As I promised, I did keep this from my Mom all those years. Funny thing is when I was about twenty six years old, my mom found out I was a witch. She asked me jokingly "Are you a good witch or a bad witch?" I laughed and said "I'm good!" Then she asked, "Can you read Tarot cards for me?" I found out that when I was a child, my Mom and my Aunt (the same Aunt who owned the fishing resort) would sneak off to have their tea leaves read on a regular basis.

When I started to learn to read Tarot cards, I began to remember things. Some things I knew were from my childhood – such as getting thrown out of my second grade class for telling a teacher her hands were green. (They were – at least the color around them was!)

But it was more things like remembering the smells of the seasons changing or knowing when it was going to rain or snow just by the scent of the air. Not being afraid of being alone, I could always sense that there was more out there, just beyond knowing – things that I could not see but I could sense.

In 1980, When I was a bit older and the same girlfriend who had taught me to read Tarot told me that she wanted the "Seth" books by Jane Roberts for her birthday, I went into the local bookstore to find them for her. I was mesmerized by the selection of books available there, even though the store was very small. But I found books about Gods and Goddesses, how to expand one's way of thinking, and books on other religions. This was all so new to me.

When I gave her the books as a birthday gift, she asked me if I had any trouble finding them. The only trouble I had was pulling myself away from that section of the bookstore.

We remained friends through our teenage years and when I was just shy of eighteen, she told me that she was going to a "party of sorts". I asked her if I could come. She made a phone call and then said it would be OK for me to go. A half hour later we pulled up in front of a house and I had no idea that I was about to attend my first Wiccan ritual. It was Beltaine 1980. Years later, I asked my friend why I was allowed to come to the ritual as I wasn't eighteen yet. Her response was that since I had married at the age of seventeen and was pregnant at the time with my first son, the Coven considered me an adult and able to make my own decisions. The answer was surprising. I now have a real hang up with underage entrance into Circle or Craft. Experience gives us wisdom and discernment.

I spent the next six months after that Beltaine ritual "pursuing" the High Priest and High Priestess of the Rite. I knew without a doubt that I wanted to be Craft. There were interviews and talks and classes. I couldn't get enough. I was in awe and wanted to learn more. I got little bits and pieces, but bits and pieces don't do it for me. Being a Virgo, I have to dig until I get it all. So I kept going back and asking questions. I was ready to do the work. I thought the High Priest and High Priestess might be put off by me because I pushed so hard, but ten days before All Hallows a Man in Black showed up at my door with a Summons. My girlfriend, knowing what was about to happen, had warned me "If a stranger shows up at your door with a letter, be respectful and don't ask any questions. Remember to offer him something to eat or drink."

The moment was both dramatic and traumatic. He's standing there holding this letter and I am speechless. I didn't want to say or do anything wrong. So he says "You may want to open that." The letter basically said this is the date set for you and this is what you need to bring and how to prepare.

I learned later that the reason my Initiation was delayed until the end of October was that I was pregnant when I asked to come into the Coven. The High Priest and High Priestess said they were unable to initiate a pregnant woman and wanted to wait until after the baby was born, . My son was due in October but arrived a few weeks early, so everything worked out. I had just enough time to recover before the event.

This was an Alexandrian Coven and I was a brand spanking new initiate with so much to learn. I started with just a basic education of the Craft - to understand what it was and why, where it came from, and how it survived through the ages. There were not only classes, but practice! And there was reading - lots of reading. And then more practice. There were years of practice and worship in the Circle during which I gained an adeptness that determined what actions were to be taken and when. It was very daunting, but oh so worth it.

At twenty-four, I achieved my Elevation to High Priestess and at twenty-six, was surprised when my Witch Queen announced her retirement and her return to England. That was the first time I can remember feeling fear in the Craft. When she left for the UK, I felt lost. But the Goddess, the Craft and my own students were waiting, and so I went on.

I am a very strict teacher. I tell my students "Don't question me, just do it." I know if they do it, it will work. I have no tolerance for whining or excuses. I would never go to my High Priestess and say "the dog ate my homework" – she would say "There's the door. Come back when you have time for us because we're making time for you."

People today think spirituality is something they can put on like new pair of pants. Our spirituality is our skin. We can never take it off – we wear it 24/7. When you treat spirituality like skin, then you understand more than you know. This is what I impress on my students and initiates. I am a tough teacher because I had a tough teacher. I tell them "You will be here. You will study at my table. You will ask questions. I expect you to ask questions."

I encourage my students to explore their own spirituality and to understand that they get to choose what happens to them. The ultimate question is when a student comes to me and asks, "Why is this happening to me?" My response to this question is "And you have allowed this, why?" This usually means they've missed something and need to go back and figure it out.

When people ask me about the Craft, I tell them I am a Priestess and a witch. When asked how I define this, I say that I am an Imparter of Older Knowledge, not ancient knowledge, as some in the greater pagan community would have people think. Our Craft is old, but how old we cannot exactly say.

I can teach only from experience and practice. All too often people misrepresent witches as the Keepers of Ancient Wisdom. I don't think this is possible considering that we do not have ancient records like cave drawings that depict the Craft. I've heard Priestesses say that things like "I am a thirteenth generation wise woman from my great-great-great-grandmother." That's nice and all, but you have to back that kind of statement up by passing the knowledge that came down to you. When you look at it in this way, you may discover that what you have is great, but not that ancient. It is part of human nature to think that the older something is, the more valuable it is. With regard to the Alexandrian tradition, Alex passed older knowledge that was revitalized through his influence.

I would liked to have met Alex. I would have said "thank you" for the inspiration I find in the Tradition and for bringing me together with other Alexandrians. These friendships are so rich and satisfying.

I definitely see perpetuation of the Craft as a part of who we are as Priests and Priestesses. It is a part of what we do. However, we do need to remember that "Many are called, but few are chosen." I feel it is up to us to find the few out of the many that will carry on that which we keep so sacred.

As a High Priestess, I teach, I train, I initiate, I elevate, and finally I hive. These aspects are very much a part not only of who I am, but of all those who have gone through these stages by my hands. Not all of them have stayed active. Not all of them have remained within the Alexandrian tradition, but all have experienced the touch of the Goddess as it was passed through either me or my Priests.

At Candlemas this year, I passed the sword to another High Priestess of the Temple and retired. I am still the primary teacher of the Temple, but no longer it's High Priestess. When I announced at Winter Solstice that I was stepping down as High Priestess of the Temple, there were a lot of tears because they thought they were losing me. I reassured them that they were not losing me but that it was time for someone else to have the experience of leading a Coven. It is a blessing to see the new High Priestess lead the Coven and to see the Coven follow.

I am reminded of the first time that I drew the sword for the Initiation of a student. It wasn't the power that I remember. It was the weight of the responsibility of knowing that from that moment on I was responsible to something much bigger than me - that I was a Priestess of the Gods and will never stop being that. I am Sovereign and I have come home. Once you become connected to the Gods, you are always connected. There is awareness that what I do somehow affects everything else, like a stone tossed in a pond. As a Priestess I am constantly plugged in and can never be separate. All that I do, all that I am, is part of that which is All.

I meet a lot of people who are coming to the Craft for the first time and who are looking for advice. I tell them not to be afraid to contact people but not just on the internet. Interact with them face to face. Get out in nature as much as possible. Remember that knowing things and understanding things are not the same. There is an old saying "When the student is ready, the teacher will come." Take it from me – the doorbell doesn't always ring. It's like the person who wants more than anything to find that special someone but who spends their days behind locked doors. You have to make things happen. You have to take action, ask the questions, and do the work.

When I look back on my life I realize that I would never have had these wonderful experiences if I didn't make it happen. It's a lot like the night I stayed out way too late in the forest and couldn't find my way home. I must have been eight years old. The American Indian children had run off but somehow I knew they were still there – hiding in the shadows – waiting to see what I would do. There was a tall tree and without even thinking about what I was doing, I went up it. I knew the forest was a dangerous place at night and that the branches of the tree would protect me and shelter me. So I scrambled up and up until I got to a place in the tree where I could rest. Sometimes life is like that. Most of the time you get home before dark and find a light has been left burning for you. But sometimes you just have to climb a tree and hold on till daylight.

Come to think of it, I've spent more than one night in a tree in this lifetime.

But I have never let go.

All the King's Children

# Green Sweets for the Green Man

*Scott*
**Third Degree High Priest**
**England**

*The young man stood quietly in the dark, facing the window. Every detail had been attended to and he was ready to begin. High above South End, the full moon shone brightly. The silver light filtered through the glass panes of the window, bathing him in shades of night. His heart beat wildly. With trembling hands, he undid the clasp on the black cloak and it fell to the floor. He stood naked within the Circle of magic he had created. Quietly at first, and then with a voice as sure as the dark, he began to read the words that would change his life forever.*

I became a born again Christian when I was eleven years old and a baptized Catholic at fourteen.

I dedicated my life to Jesus.

Yet as a boy, I was always drawn to the occult. I was fascinated by Tarot cards and loved watching horror films. This presented a big struggle within me because of my Christian walk. I tried to keep away from the occult but at the same time wanted to know more about it. Even though I had been taught that it was evil, there was something that pulled me back again and again.

When something bad happened to me, I would go to a local shop and have my Tarot cards read. I would feel really guilty afterward and would go to confession. Looking back, I don't think any of the readings were accurate. I don't remember what I thought at the time. All that mattered was having that contact. I needed to touch the cards. I knew that touching them was evil but at the same time it seemed very natural to me.

I was born in Basildon and lived on the edge of the town, surrounded by woods and country. I was always in the woods, climbing trees and enjoying nature. But I never related the language of the woods to spirituality. The forest was not a place to discover the sacred but a place to play. The church was all I knew from a very young age and I decided that when I was old enough I would take the vows of Catholic Priesthood.

The years pass quickly in a small town and I remained a devoted Christian into adulthood. I was employed as a full time Assistant Lay Pastor in my local Catholic Parish. Part of my responsibility was to act as the Youth Pastor for over 300 young people. The year was around 1991.

I began to have doubts about my faith – specifically problems with certain doctrines. I was seriously over worked at the time and thought if I could just get away for a holiday that I could recharge. So I asked the Parish Priest if I could go on retreat. He kept putting the request off until

I finally stopped asking, which further increased the personal crisis I was facing.

Then the Gulf War happened and the focus of the community changed toward the subject of warfare. As the actual war unfolded, the emphasis of the prayer community focused on a spiritual warfare. The songs we were singing started to change. One day I was listening to the words of a hymn "In Heavenly armor we enter the land, the battle belongs to the Lord" and I realized that many of the songs which should have been about God were actually about warfare. War in a spiritual sense of course - but this war was between good and evil - God and the Devil. I didn't know how I felt about this.

I was deeply entrenched in Christianity and was leading a Catholic charismatic prayer group called Act Two! I had amazing spiritual experiences while there that I can't deny. I saw people get out of wheelchairs and walk. This was a ministry of the Holy Spirit that changed people. After I became a witch I realized that miracles are possible as a result of raising power. In the prayer group we would clap and sing for hours before the healings would begin. As witches we raise that power in other ways such as dancing and chanting the Witches Rune. A different context and terminology but really the same words spoken in a different language.

At the same time that I was having these doubts about my faith, there was a big power struggle within the parish. The Parish Priest was having an affair with one of the guys in the community. Seeking someone in whom he could confide, he reached out to his sister who was also a member of the Parish. She reacted very badly to the news and proceeded to blackmail her brother. She and another Priest were keen on pushing me out of the Youth Pastor role and taking it on for themselves. This was her opportunity to do just that. She told her brother to get rid of me or she would go to the Bishop with his secret. Considering what was at stake, his decision was as I expected and I was asked to leave.

I had given my life to Jesus when I was just eleven years old. Now I felt betrayed and alone. I kept wondering if this was what divorce was like. I must have spent the next year crying and felt like I had lost a best friend.

I later got a job teaching primary school. There was another teacher at the school who I really liked. She told me she was a Pagan. I was curious about Paganism and I think she sensed this. One day she offered to lend me a book called *The Practice of Witchcraft Today*. I really wanted to read that book but found myself saying "no thank you." But I couldn't get this book out of my mind so I went back and asked her if I could still read it. She said yes, and I devoured it in one night.

I had forgotten about my connection to nature as a child, but in reading this borrowed book, I suddenly remembered being in the woods, climbing trees and picking apples. All those memories flooded back and I understood the connection between Nature and the Divine for the first time.

The book explained witchcraft differently from what I had been taught. I thought witches sacrificed babies and worshipped the devil. I now learned that this was not true and this rang some bells with me.

There were rituals in the back of the book and I decided to do a Full Moon rite. I remember I got a black cloak from the dressing up cupboard at school. On my way home I picked up bits of wood to make a fire. I was very nervous. There was no mention of the elements. But on pure instinct I put a bowl of water in the West, a feather in the East, a candle in the South, and a bowl of earth in the North. The book was very basic but I followed the ritual word by word. I lived in a block of flats on the ninth floor of an apartment building. The full moon rose that night as I had never seen it before and shone in through the windowpane. I took off the cloak and beneath it was naked. The full moon shone on me and I had the sensation of heat running through my body. From that moment on, I was hooked. I tried to go back to church. I went to confession and told the Priest that I had done a witchcraft ritual. I promised myself I would never do that again. Yet on my way home from church that night, I saw the full moon rise again and was pulled towards it. The moment I was home I was back in the Magic Circle.

The next few months were very difficult. I was going to church, but at the same time feeling pulled toward the Goddess and feeling guilty about it. I knew I had to make a choice - either the Church or Witchcraft. Before I even realized it, I had made my choice.

I tried to find a Coven or someone to talk with about the Craft but couldn't. There was no internet in 1992 and ironically I had put all of the occult shops out of business through my work with the Parish.

One morning I saw a television program about a woman who had become a pagan chaplain at a local university. I phoned the chaplain's office at the university and asked to speak with her. They were very angry that I referred to her as a chaplain. They told me "She is not a chaplain, she is a witch." Well, that made me want to speak with her even more and I begged them to give me her phone number. At first they refused but eventually they gave it to me and I rang her.

She was living in the north of England at the time and told me that she could not help me. She did suggest that I buy a copy of Prediction magazine. In the back of this magazine, I found information about the Wicca study group meeting in London, led by Vivianne and Chris Crowley. I remember going there for the first time. I was walking up the stairs to the top floor of the building and heard music coming down the corridor. I could smell incense burning. When I entered the room I saw a lot of people gathered round an altar in the middle of the room. The altar was covered with a black cloth and an athame and a chalice had been placed there. I thought "Oh my god, this really is the devil" and started to walk out. Chris Crowley saw me about to leave and came over to talk to me. He asked me to stay and I did. After attending this study group about four times, I was asked if I wanted Initiation. I said yes, and was referred to another Coven in the area.

After my Initiation, I became friends with another Priest from the Coven who lived quite near me. I went to visit him and his partner and in one of our conversations they mentioned Maxine and Alex Sanders. I didn't know anything about them at the time, so didn't give the reference much thought.

There were four initiates in my Coven and we were basically given the Book of Shadows and told to go form our own groups. I had no real training and didn't consider that I was ready to go out on my own, so the four of us decided to continue our studies together. We met at the home of one of the initiates. After a few months I thought to myself, "This is rubbish. No one knows what they are doing. No one is committed."

I was getting really discouraged. Then for some reason I remembered the reference to Maxine Sanders. I somehow knew she could help me so I worked a spell to meet her. A few days later, a copy of *Pagan Dawn* magazine arrived in the mail. Inside was an interview with Maxine. I wrote to her through the magazine and explained that I had been initiated through a Wiccan study group but had not received proper training. I patiently waited for a reply. A few days later I was telling a friend of mine about writing to Maxine and she said "I have Maxine's phone number. Why don't we just ring her?"

Maxine invited me to meet her at a pub. We had a great conversation and she later invited me to visit her at her home in Clanricade Gardens. I spent the entire afternoon and early evening with Maxine on that first visit and learned more about witchcraft in a single day than I did in the past two years. I became quite angry because what Maxine was telling me about the Craft was a completely different religion than what I was initiated into. I met with Maxine for training once a month for about a year. The last time I received training from her was the night before Lady Diana was killed. Maxine put me in touch with one of her daughter Covens so that I could continue my training. The Coven was called Temple of the Corn King.

About this same time, I was invited by Doreen Valiente to visit her in Brighton. It was ironic that for someone who once had no choices I now had two – to continue with Alexandrian Craft or to take this rare opportunity to learn Gardnerian Craft. I decided to stay with the Temple of the Corn King and am happy that I did. This was where I belonged.

I had six years of fantastic training with the Temple of the Corn King and learned some extremely hard and challenging lessons. It was not easy at all, but I fell in love with the Alexandrian tradition. I was extremely eager to find out as much about Alex as I could. In a very short period of time I saw from the training I had received that the Alexandrian tradition was one of the most beautiful expressions of Witchcraft.

In 2002 I moved to Wales to go to a university. While there I received additional training from two other Alexandrian Priestesses, Val and Wendy. Wales was a completely different ball game from London. I learned much more about the inner mysteries of the Goddess and how to be in touch with my inner self. However, after eight months in Wales, life circumstances brought me back to London. I didn't think it was right to go back to the Temple of the Corn King but wanted to continue my training.

So I ended up traveling back and forth to Wales on weekends to prepare for the higher degrees.

I was persistent and kept asking Wendy for my second and third degrees. I was told no again and again, that I was not yet ready. I was encouraged to continue my training and preparation. My education in the Craft continued for three more years until I received my second and third degrees. As it turns out, it was worth the wait. The Priestess who first initiated me into the Craft so many years ago took her third degree Alexandrian with me and we became magical partners. Together we set up the Temple of Stella Maris and began our magical work together.

I am currently running the Temple of Stella Maris, a large training Coven in London. My role as a Priest is first and foremost to serve the Gods. The second most important thing is to teach and pass on the Alexandrian tradition to others who are suitable. I take great care in training, teaching, and empowering others to higher degrees - ensuring they have really good training and that the Coven they start will be even better than this one. I want them to stand on the shoulders of their teachers the same way I do.

I never met Alex Sanders and can only go on stories that I read or have heard from people who knew him. I see Alex as the founder of our tradition, someone who was a channel for the Goddess. He enabled a different expression of the Craft. He was a wonderful man and I'm sure a very naughty boy. I really wish that I had met him.

For many years, every Beltaine we would attend a May Day celebration in Oswestry, Shropshire. The celebration was usually held in the fields but one year all of England was suffering from an outbreak of the "foot and mouth" disease, so May Day celebration was restricted to the town. That was the year I was chosen to be the famous Oswestry Green Man. I traveled up to Shropshire to Wendy's home. The women of the Coven dressed me in the Green Man costume. When I was ready, three Priestesses invoked the God on me.

I remember how nervous I was – walking down the middle of the street dressed in green – my face hidden by a mask. We passed different car parks on the way to the May Pole. People stood staring at me. I was expected to dance and get people going. The problem was that inside my costume, behind the mask of a God, I felt very human. I tried to dance but got very tired. We then moved down the road a bit to the main site, which was on top of a hill. Children came running out of nearby houses asking for green sweets from the green horn of the Green Man. Suddenly I was no longer me. The power of the God took hold of me and I started to dance. I was this Being who was talking and laughing with the children. I was still there but very much in the background. I was dancing with the children and gave them candy and then we went to another site and I danced some more. In the back of my head I was asking myself "Where are you? Where have you gone?"

When we finished we went to the pub and I took off the mask. The power gradually drained away and I came back to the forefront. Later I realized that I had danced for over eight hours without stopping. The next day I couldn't go to school. I literally couldn't move my legs. This was the most amazing, powerful, and moving experience of the God that I had so far.

It changed me completely.

I hear many people say that it is most important in life to believe in one's self. Life can be difficult at times. I think to believe in yourself, you first need someone to believe in you. As much as I want to think I can press forward and keep going, I know that unless there is someone who believes in me, I can't do it.

Wendy, the High Priestess who brought me to the higher degrees, believed in me and saw my potential, and for that I will always love her. Because of her, I became the High Priest the Goddess wants me to be. If not for her faith in me, I probably would have quit. She said "I believe in you. Do this. Trust the magic and see what happens."

Each initiate I bring into the Craft has brought upon me this weight of responsibility. I keep thinking to myself "Am I worthy? Do I know enough? Can I lead them?"

Before my second and third degrees I was quite arrogant. After I became a High Priest I realized the truth - that I know nothing and would never stop learning. Teaching is a responsibility. There is joy in it but there is also self-reflection. The more I learn, the more I am reminded that I know nothing.

I believe in my students the same way that Wendy believed in me. I want to hold them up when they think they can't go on. Teaching makes me humble. This is the safety key to stop my ego from going off the wall. When I see my initiates take control of the Circle, I step back from being active and watch them proudly. My heart sings with joy.

I am grateful to Alex and Maxine. They did all the groundwork so we can have this beautiful and wonderful tradition. I am Alexandrian and I wouldn't want to be anything else.

# By Hand of Write

*Radella*
**Third Degree High Priestess**
**Canada**

*I* am grateful to Jimahl for inviting my participation in his book. I find myself humbled in sharing my story within the Craft. I have so very much yet to learn and many days I feel that I am still at the beginning. I wonder how I will later reflect on my words when I have grown further and faced transformations to come.

For me, it began in 1979, at the end of high school. I found Linda Goodman's book, *Sun Signs*, in a local library and loved it. I signed out a book on how to cast astrology charts and began experimenting on family, friends and local professionals. Shortly after, I read about the Tarot, bought a deck, and starting reading for others. In the same library section, I found Sybil Leek, Gerald Gardner, and Margot Adler. I devoured all of the occult books the library stocked. I read books on psychic skills and began practicing their exercises. I was still young. So, I made a promise to myself that I wouldn't seek a Coven until I had time to settle my location, my identity, and my life. It was a hard promise, but it was a promise that I kept.

I first heard of Alexandrian witchcraft in reading Margot Adler's *Drawing Down the Moon*. That same year, in the biography section of the library, I discovered June Johns' book on Alex Sanders' life and Craft, *King of the Witches*. It seemed pretty sensational, but I recognized an aspect from the other authors I had read. Here was someone else claiming to be a witch – not all that different than Sybil Leek or Gerald Gardner. This gave me a sense that there were multiple pathways into the Craft and yet they all shared a certain seriousness about them. To be a part of this required dedication – that was what I was looking for. It's interesting now to look back and realize that it would be another twenty years from this moment before I met an Alexandrian. There was an initial recognition of something that seemed familiar, then a long disconnect - and then re-discovery.

I was born in a small town Canadian community. The town was situated within an agricultural paradise and rather renowned for its natural splendor. The area was marked by migrations, fresh waters, forest, and a direct relationship to food production.

My parents were very down to earth. They loved to simply camp in a trailer, travel provincial roads and explore, sit around a campfire in the night air, share a cup of cocoa, and play cards. My Dad began with very little in life. He grew up on the waters and found his serenity in nature. My Mom grew up in a large family. She found her joy in laughing and in her siblings.

Our times together were drives to see the deer, the ducks, the birds, the smelting. We listened to the crickets, the geese, the crows, the grasshoppers, and the toads.

I'm not sure I was especially occult-oriented in early childhood. I loved animals and being in nature, especially near water. I collected rocks and enjoyed quiet time. I was very animistic, ascribing life to most things around me. I can recall having a superstitious leaning, following simple rules of luck. I had a rather busy imagination, which later was a useful tool in the Craft.

I miss the potential of youth and sharpness of learning. I read books related to witchcraft in late adolescence. But, there are so many areas I now wish I'd studied then to prepare me for my Craft now: animal behavior, nature lore, plant identification, mythology, geography, geology, meditation, history, anthropology. If I was in high school again, I might research more of astronomy, soil, bird calls, human physiology, insects, chemistry. I might take music, voice, or dance lessons. Youth should be a time to indulge in knowledge.

My parents were Christian and religious in their own individual expressions. My mother was spiritual, holding her religion close to her heart in a quiet way. She believed that the relationship with God was a personal one and most honestly expressed in private. My father's religious commitment was deeply genuine and very personal. He enjoyed attending church, albeit it occasionally, and spoke very gently about what it meant to him. I realized only after he had died that he was the one who instilled in me a spiritual core. He modeled an internal dedication and approached his religion as nourishing.

I did not attend church with my father in adult years. In hindsight, I sometimes wish I had. When he was dying, it was his prayers I spoke to him and his Bible I read at the funeral, with true sincerity and connection. I never felt so much a Priestess of my own religion as I did in passing him through the Veil with his.

I did not feel alienated from Christianity. It still feels like a warm friend that is welcome to visit. The Wicca was something I felt called to seek, rather than something alternative. I wasn't looking to escape my childhood religion; I was looking for the home I knew was beckoning.
Like many others, my first magic circles were solitary. I was excited at the opportunity to attend a public Halloween ritual at a university. However, most attendees were curious observers and the Circle was cast for demonstration. It was the beginning of a lifetime journey, but my first exposure to ritual was educational rather than magical.

Not long after, a co-worker introduced me to Reclaiming, which was an extension of Starhawk's work. It was here that I had my first small Circle surrounded by witches. This Circle wasn't drawn for the sake of observers. It was cast with intent through the knife that I had lent. What I had read in books was now vibrating through my body. It was almost like falling in love, as I realized that this was the commitment I wanted for life. This led to a period of circling within this Tradition, in Covens, in community, and spontaneously with friends. I began to watch TV specials on witches and feel like I was one. But, those same TV shows often left me yearning for a Traditional Initiatory Coven. I didn't quite feel like I had yet found the world that Sybil, Gerald, and Alex had toured me through.

My first group circle within a Traditional context was an outer court ritual hosted by local Georgians, nearly 20 years ago. The Georgian Priesthood remains dear to me, for being the first to let me dance the round of a Traditional Craft. That led to me joining an outer court Coven that was Gardnerian-led, where I studied for three years. It was 14 years after I had read Gardner and was the Craft I had been waiting for. I felt alive, whole, ignited, and vibrant. I felt a deep closeness to the Rites and to the people, from the moment Circle was cast. I felt meaning. I felt right. It became the candle that lit my way to my Alexandrian Craft. I still count the Georgians and my prior Coven Priesthood among my Elders and close friends.

Seeking was a circuitous route of speed bumps and patience for me. True to my promise to take my time, nothing happened quickly. I read my first Craft book at seventeen and took my First Degree Initiation into a British Columbia eclectic Tradition twenty years later. Over the past ten years, I have taken oaths in the three degrees, hived my coven, and passed the rites onward. I would not have my Craft as it is today if not for the High Priestess of this Tradition opening a door.

At age 39, I took my Oath by Alexandrian rite and at 41, I deepened to Second Degree. When I was 44, I Initiated my students to First Degree and hived my Alexandrian Maiden Coven, carrying our line from Ontario and Connecticut to British Columbia. At 44 years old, I was warmly welcomed into the Sublime Third Degree by loving Alexandrian kin and witnessing Gardnerian Elders. My High Priestess housed traveling visitors and hosted a party of Initiates and friends. I felt utterly showered. It had been worth every minute of waiting and searching. It was as if a long shiver had finally come to rest.

I appreciate and maintain my relationships with all of my Initiatory pathways. Every one of them has helped to form me. Every one of them is family. But each is distinct and I do not blend my British Traditional Wicca and eclectic practices. I very much believe in passing the Tradition as I was passed it, without diffusion or obscurity.

I try to discuss with new seekers the importance of not rushing into life altering decisions. Changing a religion is a major transformation and should not be undertaken lightly or rashly. I like to encourage seekers to learn about different traditions, to sample, to meet other Covens and Priesthood before they Initiate. It is important that a Coven and its Elders be a compatible and trusted fit.

I find talking about how I view my role as a High Priestess very difficult. It is not easy to articlate how I feel because it is now so deeply a part of me. The Circle that was once cast around me is now inscribed inside of me.

When I raise my tool to cast a Circle, it is not just performing an act. It is something in which my whole being is partaking. It's not a drawing hand anymore – it's a heart that comes forward through the tip of the blade. That Circle was cast around me when I was initiated and around my initiator when he was initiated. I cast the same Circle around my students when I initiate. It all becomes a part of an imprint into family. Every time I raise my tool I am re-inscribing the Circle that has been put inside me. Every Sabbat and every Esbat, I am aware that the Circle is being cast elsewhere by people who are kin, who are speaking the same words and doing it the same way. As a result I am never casting alone – a thousand hands go around the Circle on multiple layers and places.

We are a religion without followers. We serve our Gods as their Priesthood. Every ritual is participatory and every celebrant must come prepared. To be a Priestess, whether leading the Circle or attending, is to be fully ready to engage, to generate energy, to expend effort. As a Priestess, it means that I need to ensure the ritual has purpose, place, and resources. It is a work on the mundane as much as the arcane. In the Circle, I raise magic. Before the Circle, on nights I host, I am simply "HPS, House and Potty Scrubber", first among equals.

Initiation triggers a process of growth. The mysteries teach us and change us. To walk through the Gate is to confront fear and to not only become the Hidden, but to face the hidden within one's self. My role as a Priestess is to allow myself to see, to sense, beyond, beneath, around, behind. It is to open, past the obvious, lift the veil, and be touched by greater mysteries. It is to be challenged, de-constructed, re-built, re-aligned, and shaped into a tool that lovingly fits the hands of the Gods. It is to honor the transformative face of the Lady by letting myself be transformed.

We are a life affirming religion. We are not only participatory in ritual, but in life. We know, with certainty, that rebirth follows death. As a Priestess, I cannot allow the mini-deaths of life to end my cycle of growth, learning, becoming. Sometimes transformations are welcome; sometimes they are painful. My role is to learn within the cauldron of change. It is to rejoice, not simply to survive. Our Gods are happy when we are happy.

My relationship with the Gods is somewhat like being in love. When we are apart, I hunger for Their company. When we are together, I rejoice and feel whole. And so, I honor the relationship with a sense of commitment, tenderness, honesty, self-reflection, and mutuality. I offer gifts and I receive gifts, exchanged in fondness. Like someone I cherish, I let Them know that They are thought of, remembered, familiar, and welcome. I honor them in the way that they love and answer.

As a Priestess, I have learned that in the silence of the night, I can hear Their heartbeat and know They are alive. The Gods of the Wicca are not omnipotent. They need us as we do Them. My role is to show Them love and life. Our Gods are the type of guests who prefer an invitation before stopping by. If we never invite Them, then the relationship fades away. When we regularly invite Them to family holidays, then the relationship is stronger and They are stronger. They, like any of us, are at our best when cherished.

The Craft has flourished since Gerald and Alex. We are working, teaching, hiving. We're across continents. We've grown into traditions, lines, and lines within lines. As a result, I do not see my role as a High Priestess to perpetuate as much as I do to preserve the Craft.

I believe that role is to simultaneously preserve the Wicca and the Craft of the Wicca. That means, for me, that Initiating new witches is not enough. They must be witches who experience, and who pass our core rites and lore. As Alexandrian, I share the mysteries at Initiations and through our rituals. A part of what I believe is that these are passed in subtle ways, through the nuances of wording, gesture, timing, and the body itself. As a result, I honor that even small changes can imprint the candidate in discernible and pronounced ways. As I entrust them with my Craft, I know they trust me with what they will receive. Preserving, for me, means I fulfill that trust and that they will fulfill it in turn with their candidates.

In doing Initiations, we do not just follow a script, we follow a groove. We re-enact what we ourselves have had etched within. A part of my role is to carve that groove with precision, ensuring it is a road that can be found again in the future when the Initiate becomes the Initiator. It is that road that we each experience in our own way but that we pass on with a common map.

What is most important to me is not the quantity of the Wicca but the quality of the Wicca. It is to develop leaders, critical thinkers, and capable witches. It is to work toward a generation of witches that is stronger than our own, that the Craft may prosper.

My Coven is currently the only lineaged Alexandrian Coven operating in British Columbia. I know that if my Coven does not continue, the Wicca will. My aim, then, is not expansion, but to do the work rightly. We have seeded an Alexandrian current that is humbly blooming with the fragrance of a west coast rose. For those who find that aroma awakens them we open the threshold to the Circle and share the map. At the end of the day, though, healthy planting relies upon the land. We will only plant roses so long as the soil of British Columbia is fertile and only as many as the soil is able to grow. If we fade away, we have still danced with the Gods and, hopefully, given them joy.

It's been 30 years since I began my interest in the Craft. My training has never been a streamlined route. I've wound in a spiral getting to the Wicca. It's like trying to summarize the lines of a jigsaw puzzle. It all fits together when complete, but it's a long and seemingly disjointed story to talk about the pieces.

I've circled solitary, in small informal eclectic covens, in communities, and in outer courts. I've received valuable teachings from Georgian, New Reformed Orthodox Order of the Golden Dawn, Gardnerian, and eclectic Elders. I've received one-on-one mentoring from eclectic and ceremonial witches, in operative magic and ritual.

I spent over two years exchanging ideas and coming to know my Alexandrian High Priestess before I Initiated. I am one of the witches who had to travel many miles to answer that unrelenting call of the Wicca. My Initiators and Coven were across the country. There have been many long distance three-hour phone calls and visits. We've exchanged lengthy emails multiple times per week; we've set up e-groups for kin. My High Priestess has hosted me for a week to three weeks at a time, offering intense immersion and copying time. I've flown in for my own Initiations, to witness Initiations, to perform rituals. I've written rituals for my coven to conduct and test in my absence. In establishing my own Coven, it has been necessary to fly in Elders and High Priesthood to assist with and witness downline Initiations. It has been worth every penny, every stumbling block, and every mile.

My High Priestess has kept the pace with me though all the bumps and challenges. In doing so, she has ensured that my own Coven members have a place nearby where they can come.

I am currently very happily active as the High Priestess of RosenHearth Coven. I am surrounded by good Craft family, both immediate and extended. I have wonderful people in my Circle and it's a joy to gather with them.

As a Coven, we try to walk with a whisper, doing the work within moonlit shadows. But, we have strong caring ties with other local traditions and community. The British Columbia pagan community has a long history of diverse paths coming together throughout the year.

From the moment I entered the Initiatory Circle, my Elders shared their most important gift: Trust. It was the Trust to value, to study, to honor, to protect what their Elders had previously entrusted to them. They opened what they held most sacred. They taught me with love, with care, and with friendship. They honored me as family.

What I have been given is, to me, like an inherited treasure. My hope for a family heirloom would be to hold it with the same heart and appreciation as it has been held before. It would be to add more love to it, keep it polished, learn all I can about it, and pass along its stories. It would be to ensure each story is told, intact, with the same flavor, the same detail, undistorted. My hope would be to choose mindfully its next inheritors, that it never come to harm or loss, and that it would be passed in entirety. I would want to feed it, nurture it, admire it, and study it for understanding. I would want to see its richness and full essence, that I may know within why my family has so cherished it. I would want it to teach me about myself and who I am. I would want to both unveil its purpose and fulfill it. Most importantly, I would want to pass it along, to the next generation, knowing that it will carry on and that the family will carry on.

It is my hope that, like the heirloom, I will keep my Craft in trust, for the Wicca of the past and the Wicca of the future. And when seekers approach the Gate and feel like family, I will pass what was passed to me, with the same love and care.

My training has impressed upon me that I am part of a network. As I am offering my words, I do not and cannot speak for or represent anyone but myself. The Wicca are autonomous. Yet, I am also very aware that I carry with me my Elders, Initiates, and Coven wherever I go. Being a part of the Wicca means I do not ever walk alone. That brings with it the great benefit of connection. Our voices are intertwined with each ritual, across the miles. That bond also means that I bear responsibility and accountability, to the Gods we serve and the Wicca who have embraced me. Our Circles are separate and our Circles are conjoined.

Within my magic, I use my training to beckon the God. To tease illusion and ego apart from truth that I may hear untainted the Lady's whisper. To spin the wheel and let the mysteries take me through life and death, becoming my moral compass. To gather when the moon is bright, to teach and meet, to dance and sing. To work the Arts and do the spells of our Craft, for health, wealth, strength, fertility, and joy. To fulfill the call of Priesthood, by the specific rites of our Gods, honoring the pact between us. To feed Them as They feed me with the fuel of life. To know my loved ones, and to know that we will meet again.

I have never known Alex. So, for me, it is much like dining around the table with close relatives in a childhood family. I am with those whom I have gotten to know and love, and who know me well. We will tell many stories about grandmothers and grandfathers that I never met. Aunts and uncles will share with me what previous generations were like. I will feel a warmth in my heart and be able to remark on similarities throughout the family. It will make me feel like part of a chain and give me a place in the world. They will tell me stories of quirks, some exaggerated for entertainment, some minimized to save grace, some told in humor to celebrate beloved characters. As they speak, I will feel a love deep inside for one whom I have never met, but who nonetheless made me who I am, quirks and all. At times, I will strongly wish I could have met this relative who created my family and taught the parents, aunts, uncles, siblings, and cousins who have in turn taught me. Instead, even among those who knew him, a now passed relative remains a mystery, known only through the link and the experience of what customs he has contributed to the family.

I have much the parallel sentiments about Alex. I find myself often reading the stories and words of those who knew him, with hunger and eager ears. I listen for warmth in the telling and I glean seeds of who he might have been. Inside me develops a very special spot, as I look to my Kin and realize that we are related through him. Without ever having known him, I have inherited a gift from him - family bonds, a place ever to turn, a Circle of love. And, so, I sense him, no longer as an anonymous legend, but as someone I have gotten to know through the magic that links us.

While I may not know Alex or who he really was as a man, there is something of him that I feel every time I stand in Circle with "our people."

I know him through the experience of what customs he has contributed to the family. He is the style of carving the turkey and making the gravy that has been passed from generation to generation that we will not change because it is "us". My immediate kin are those who share the table with me, hug me when we meet and greet, and ensure the turkey is cooked that I may never hunger. They are the ones, who in their stories, carefully teach me that special style of carving the turkey and making the gravy. And we return every holiday to do it again, simply because it is home.

I think it's important to remember that what we've inherited from Alex is a legacy, not an icon. It is tempting to idealize him, with generations between us. But, Alex remains to me a man, in his flaws, his frailties, his ethical highs and lows, his fears, his mistakes. The benefit of having Elders is not that they pass us the wisdom of their perfection. It's that they pass us the wisdom gained from being human. I am grateful for Alex, for both his wisdoms and his humanity.

"Keep a book in hand of write…"

One of the most significant moments of my life occurred after I had hived my Coven. It is the first time one of my Initiates visited and sat at the kitchen table, candle lit, incense burning. She opened her newly acquired Book of Shadows, blank, awed by the moment upon her. I laid my own Book in front of her and turned to the first page.

In that instance, we were together and time stood still. She put her pen to paper and began to carve out the words. It was no longer just the words, but an imbued spell. It was a core thread that ran through us all. She was tracing that thread as I had before her, as my initiators had, and as their initiators had. I knew that there would soon be a time that she would pick up her tool to carve the Circle as I had carved it and our Elders had carved it. These words and that moment would merge together. Perhaps one day, she would repeat that moment with her own Initiate. That experience has repeated for me with every member of my Coven. We are larger than the book we write, but we are also bound through its pages, stained in Circle and opened with trust.

We are the Priesthood of the Mysteries. They re-make us, with each encounter. A cake mixed, beaten, and baked cannot be returned to its original raw ingredients.

My service to the Wicca and the Craft is in this life and the next. It has promised me return and to know love again. I cannot quit rebirth and it would be a very lonely reward to try.

One of the most difficult experiences of my life was an invitation to Initiate that I did not fulfill. I faced the time afterwards, solitary, feeling lost and homeless. I felt deeply hollow. I realized in that time that no challenge I could face in pursuing my Craft would ever be greater than the loss of being without it. I learned that when the Gate opens, the Gods are waiting for entry. I learned that I am part of a grander Craft; my Craft is not about me. I discovered that there is a time to serve and the timing is not necessarily mine.

The Craft has called for a place in my life, as it has for many of the Wica. We make choices about career goals, housing, relationships, hobbies, activities, family, and friends. Our Sabbats are merriment, yet they also teach us about the grimy blood of slaughter, physical labor in the fields, hardship, hunger, gratitude, going without, fear, and hard choices. The Initiatory path can bring its own Abyss, but I have learnt to trust where the magic is taking me.

There is always a new sense of ecstasy behind the next curtain.

Journey to Nirvana


*Paul Hardy*
**Third Degree High Priest**
**England**

*I*n about 1967, whilst walking through my local market, I realized God.

I can remember the moment very clearly. It wasn't a revelation. There were no angels singing from heaven. Just a pure, solid realization of the inner connectedness of everything. A single thought in which everything becomes one thing. I called it God because that's what I thought then and would still think the same now. But because I was brought up in a non-religious family that transition was personally a surprise.

It came out of the blue. From that moment on, I realized there was another language or another life that had existed all the while that I hadn't seen - a life to which I had been blind.

I was seventeen years old and this experience spurred me to start reading. I was drawn to Buddhism, primarily because Christianity never rang any bells. I looked to the Eastern religions partly because in the sixties, Buddhism was one of the only alternative religions around. Buddhism fit into the humanity of the era. Personally I found resonance within teachings of Buddha and Islam. It wasn't until a couple of years later that I came across concepts of Craft.

It was about that time that I read *King of the Witches* by June Johns. I had developed a deep fascination with mythology and folklore from early childhood so to find something contemporary which resonated in a folkloric way fit me well. Reading this book opened many doors.

I contacted Alex from a post office box number in the back of the book. I was a very shy child and struggled with this shyness even as a young man. But I was sincerely interested in learning more, so I wrote Alex a letter. This was so unlike me. In response, I received a brochure of occult jewelry made by a local craftsman. The brochure was nice, but occult jewelry wasn't what I needed. So I took a trip to the jeweler and asked him if he could help put me in touch with Alex Sanders.

He looked at his watch and then nodded toward the street. "If you hurry, you can probably catch him having a pint at the White Swan Pub."

I rushed off to the pub and sure enough found Alex sitting there. I introduced myself and he received me into his company. It rolled from there.

I was invited to attend dictation and lecture which were held twice a week. This went on for a good number of months. Because I was a non-initiate, I was not permitted to attend Circle. On these nights, the Coven would go off to Circle and I would stay behind in the pub and wait for them to return. So I had the social side but not the working side.

Knowing that at some point I was going to take Initiation, I carried my three Initiation cords in my bag so I would have them with me when the moment came. One Thursday night I showed up expecting lectures and Alex said "You're going to be initiated tonight." There was no time to prepare.

He took me back to his flat where I assumed the Initiation would take place. But nothing seemed prepared there. Alex always traveled with an entourage and on this night there were at least forty people crowded into the flat. Suddenly I heard the sound of coaches pulling up in front and everyone filed out of the flat onto these buses.

No one said anything about where we were going and the coaches headed off into the night. I had no idea what was going to happen. We drove through the dark for over two hours before the coaches pulled off the main road onto a country track. Eventually this country road ended and we had to get out of the bus and start walking up a lane. Finally we came to an old English manor house that looked deserted and neglected. No one said anything, they just kept moving along. We entered the house through a back door and walked silently through empty hallways. It was like a Hammer horror film set. At the end of one of these long corridors we entered a large room where a Circle had been prepared. This was where I was initiated. It was absolutely stunning and far better than anything I could have dreamed up.

As it turned out, this was a triple Initiation of myself and two other Priests. We were each assigned a Priestess to take us through the Initiation while Alex and Maxine presided. I received my scourging, from Alex the final stroke and this was not one I'll ever forget.

I remember there were so many people attending meetings in London, within the Circle everyone stood shoulder to shoulder. There was just enough room for Alex to push by people to cast the Circle. This is how it always was when working with Alex and Maxine. There was a continuous influx of people. Some were members of the original Covens; some were visiting from other Covens. There were numerous visitors from overseas. It was a wild time.

Following my Initiation, it took me time to recover and earth myself. It was an extraordinary event. I had no doubt of the seriousness of the step I was taking – I was one step closer to the Divine.

I was born in London. My Father was a Socialist humanist and gave me and my brothers a good grounding in other belief systems. My

Mother gave me an insight into the magical world.

She was not directly connected with magic as you and I would understand it, but she had contact with a few mediums in childhood. She also had a fairy experience. As children we found the stories about faeries interesting. I remember asking her to re-tell me the faery story which reaffirmed the reality of the magical world to me.

When you go to school these myths start to break down because they are not reinforced by teachers and broader society. My mother was a sounding block where I could go back and hear stories which balanced my need for the mysterious world. My mother would not speak of such things when my father was around, so I had to wait until he was at work. This was a private world between me and my mother. I associate these memories with sitting on her lap and feeling her softness. My father found physical contact difficult. Sitting with my mother and listening to her stories over and over gives me that love in the heart that I associate with the Great Mother – like going home to a hug and knowing you will always be accepted back regardless of what a bastard you've been.

As much as we were a non-religious household we had a fundamental belief in the sacred. We just never went to churches. My father traveled in the Navy during the Second World War. His travels took him into the Near East so he picked up a lot of information on Buddhism and Karma. He would discuss these principles with my brother and me at a young age. I was able to understand the concept of brotherly love because we are all humans but the spirit wasn't in it. My father read the Bible to us but we discussed it from an anthropological and scientific point of view, rather than a religious one.

My brother and I were very close. As brothers, we told each other everything. After I was initiated, I shared the experience with him. He came into the Craft a year or so later.

I stayed with Alex and Maxine for approximately a year which brought them close to the separation point. It was not as easy as it had been and in some ways I think Alex had hit a bit of a wall. This is a purely personal observation. He had tried the "rock and roll" road but after a number of attempts found it difficult to move to that next step. He yearned to go to America but those things seemed to be blocked to him. Then the break-up occurred. Whenever a High Priest and High Priestess split up, the Coven sometimes splits as well. There was a sense of panic and I stopped going regularly for training. After Alex went to Sussex, Maxine pulled the Temple back together and my brother was initiated.

I had moved out of London by 150 miles, so traveling in and out of the city wasn't so easy. I started studying Qabbalah and other forms of magic. I became quite adept at these things but as much as I could talk magic and work Craft, I couldn't initiate. So I finished my training and took my second and third degrees from a Shropshire based Temple that had connections with my brother's Coven in London.

When I was a young man, I saw the Priesthood as a very different thing than I do now. I think that we were closer to the old times then. I say "we" in the context of Alexandrian witches.

I don't know how much of this is my own internal shaping or flavoring, but in many ways the Craft world then was very, very small. People read serious works like the Key of Solomon, and Agrippa. There was a lot of study and social discussion. All of the references were of the past – we worked with the imagery of a much older version. I read God of the Witches by Margaret Murray when she was considered to be an honest anthropological writer. Since that time, she's been pulled to pieces. That direct connection with our most ancient lineage has been muddled over the years. Who would have imagined that Margaret Murray would not fit into the modern neo-pagan mold?

I take an active role in the perpetuation of the Craft but also realize that as a Magician I have a responsibility to humanity.

I see the spiritual journey of myself as an extension of humanity. The journey of the spirit is to achieve oneness with Godhead, whichever path you walk. I have chosen the Craft as the vehicle but my philosophies are not restricted to Craft in a narrow form. As a magician and as a High Priest and Magus, my personal work is in understanding myself and my relationship to the universe.

Every individual that clarifies themselves clarifies for humanity. Every soul that reaches Nirvana, lifts all of humanity with it. As a High Priest of the Craft, I must always remind myself that my journey is not only my journey, but one I share with all others. It is important to keep pure my highest ideals and to always try to improve the lot of my fellow man. In the mundane world I am an artist. On my spiritual path I am also an artist. The same vocation, just working with different tools.

When I think of Alex, I remember his very sad eyes and his beautiful soft voice. You would reveal everything to him within seconds of meeting him. He was not demanding in any hard and fast way. He allowed you to be. He had great style. He knew how to present himself. He knew how to walk into a room. He had a sort of softness and a great gentleness.

He was not a very tall or big man but he would fill a space completely. He had remarkable charisma and a very wicked sense of humor. His school boy pranks endeared him to people. He could take the most mundane occasion and make it extraordinary. He had strength and power but never dominated with it. You most certainly would take notice if he said something. He would have bent over backwards for you. In the broader sense he was that embodiment of King of the Witches. On a personal level he had great problems. But he was the King of the Witches and he died a King and left us with this wonderful sort of family. I am a creator of myths and see things in mythic terminology. I see Alex very much as the reluctant king - willingly going to his doom.

For a while I was actually embarrassed to say I was Alexandrian because he was taking such a lot of flack. This was partly my immaturity and not fully understanding what was going on. By returning to myself and accepting my Alexandrian tradition, I stand up alongside Alex as I think many of us do.

I ask for understanding. My part in that is to keep striving to understand, even when what I understand is hard.

Understanding can be extremely unnerving and unsettling. When we say show me the truth and the truth is shown to us it may destroy the images we rely upon and that is a scary place. But ultimately I've asked to see it and it is my duty to move forward even when I don't want to. My personal "want to" is obviously flawed – especially when you stand on the brink of something and see its vastness and are dumbfounded by it.

When I think back to discovering God in the marketplace, I suppose God is the act of creation in the Kether concept. Something beyond shaping or understanding by its nature. Our God and Goddess are emanations of that. The twin pillars are dual forces, male and female. All pantheons lead back to one source, so does everything else. A journey of spirit is a journey of creation. There is only one creation. Words and symbols are personal reflections of one Unity.

Sunset on the Nile - photo taken by Kore on the evening of her
Egyptian Initiation

# Born into Magic

*Kore Pendragon*
**First Degree Priestess**
**England**

*It is perhaps a characteristic of good writing that very few stories ever truly begin at the beginning. But in telling Kore Pendragon's story, there is no other way to start. As it turns out, Kore is the closest one could ever come to a hereditary Alexandrian witch. Both of Kore's parents were initiated and trained by Alex and Maxine Sanders and were members of the original London Coven.*

There hasn't been a point in my life where I haven't been in Wicca. I believe that I may have been in Wicca or something like it in a past life as well. My mother told me that when I was very young, about three years old I told her that I remembered being chased by people who looked very much like the medieval Witchunters, who caught me and beat me to death. As I was very little at the time I had not been told about any persecution as she didn't want to frighten me. I don't have these memories any more thankfully.

I was born into a magical family. The first time I entered a magic Circle was my wiccaning at three weeks of age. The very next time I stepped into a proper working Circle was on the eighteenth anniversary of my wiccaning, when I was initiated as a witch. I was always allowed to go into the Circle for the Sabbats, which I loved, but not for any ritual or magical work.

I think some people assume because my parents were both witches that I never had a personal choice in deciding my spiritual path. Nothing could be farther from the truth. When I was a child I went to a Church of England primary school. I was exposed to Christianity from a very early age. At any point in my life I could have chosen a Christian or other path. As an adult I am deeply moved and influenced by the Gnostic Gospels and consider them to be a major part of my understanding of the Mysteries. When people ask me why I came back to Wicca at the age of eighteen, I say "I never left it to begin with." I learned as much as I could about other religions but never considered not being a witch. It's always been there. There has never been a point when I haven't been Wicca. It was at that time when I was in primary school that I first became aware of ancient Egypt. We were studying it at school, I started drawing pictures of the Egyptian Gods and Goddesses and from that moment I was completely hooked. When I came home and told my mother that we were studying ancient Egypt, she told me that this was her first great love and that she and my father had become friends whilst in Alex and Maxine's Coven because of their mutual love of Egypt, its Gods and mysteries. I don't consider Wicca to be the one and only way to truth but that all other spiritual paths, including all contemporary religions, contain the inner knowledge if you look for it. My ideas about Wicca are coloured by what I learn from the Ancient Egyptians and it is Egypt that I consider to be my true spiritual home.

*Kore was able to communicate with spirits from a young age and to understand things which are hidden from many others. The world of spirits was just as real to her as the material world around her. Fortunately for Kore she grew up in a supportive home where her parents were more interested in providing her with free choice than making decisions for her about what has value and what does not.*

I remember talking about the spirits to my mother and being told that they are wise beings who are there to help us learn. One night I was standing next to my mother brushing my teeth. There was a pile of towels on the side and I asked her if the spirits would do things to frighten me like throw the towels on the floor. I didn't mind the spirits but was nervous of them moving things. My mother said the spirits didn't do things like that. At that moment the stack of towels promptly flew to the floor. We both laughed and I wasn't frightened after that. Later I learned that that they often move things around for some reason, just not always right in front of me.

I remember one Christmas Eve where my mother and I were coming out of a store where we had been last minute shopping. There was one particular spirit my mother is very close to and she had forgotten to buy him a Christmas present. Well he didn't like that at all. The car ignition turned on and off repeatedly. The only problem was our friend in whose car we were had the keys in her hand! My mother realised what he was trying to tell her, turned around and headed back to the store to buy him the present.

We are often aware that many spirits are with us in our home. I often say that if we could touch and feel all the spirits in this place we would not be able to move in this house. This perception of the world of spirits is not unusual to me. The fact that some people aren't aware of the spirits seems peculiar.

People also assume, because I was born into a witch family, that I lived some sort of enchanted life or that I spent my childhood in a fairy tale world. I was actually quite normal. When I was little I wanted to be a test pilot when I grew up. Then I wanted to be an astronaut. My bedroom was not filled with fantasy posters but with anything related to NASA and Space. I had models of a Saturn V, and space shuttle hanging from the ceiling. Even today I have a painting of an Apollo space Craft on my wall that was painted for me by my spiritual father Chris.

My mother must have told me about Alex Sanders from an early age; however I do remember being taken to see him when I was very young, I remember seeing a man sitting in a chair, smiling. I think he may have been eating chocolate marzipan which my mother had taken for him. He was very nice and in my eyes he seemed tall, which he wasn't. I must have been very short as I only came up to about his knees. I was about three or four years old. I didn't hear his voice again until years later when my mother played me a recording (A Witch is Born). I have had several dreams about him where he has given me advice on things relevant to Wicca to share with my mother.

My father left when I was nine but I have really happy memories of childhood. Despite my father leaving I did have a father figure in my life, Chris who was also an Alexandrian Priest and my mother's best friend. Sadly he is no longer with us. He used to take me for walks when I was little and talk to me about Wicca and the Gods. When I was older he would always be there for me whenever I needed any help or advice. A few days after he died he came to visit me in a dream to reassure me that all was well. He's been to see me several times since and though I miss him dearly, I know we will meet up again and he is always a part of my life and our Circle.

When I was very young I wasn't allowed to know anything about the workings of magic. I think partly for my own protection and also so I didn't let slip any information while playing with my friends or at school. And you can't have a small child in a ritual where you need total concentration or in rituals where the people may be skyclad. At that time there was a lot of stuff in the newspapers about the fictitious 'satanic abuse of children' and plenty of people had their children taken into care as a result.

All I was told was not to say anything about the people who were in the Coven or to talk about wicca. My parents didn't want to frighten me and the less I knew the less damage could be done. But even now I understand that there is more advanced information than I should have at my current level of training. Just recently I was with my mother in a shopping mall and she started to say something about the inner meaning of a higher Initiation and then stopped and said "Sorry I can't tell you that.

You're not ready."

Once when I was a girl I tried my hand at a bit of magic just to see what would happen. It produced dodgy results. Everyone in the house got sick and spent the night in the bathroom. Later my mother asked "Have you been doing moon magic?" I had!

One time my mother and I were sitting in a van on the outside of Windsor Great Park. These are the Queen's grounds and closed to the public. There was an ancient oak tree there called Herne's Oak. We had set out to take the tree an offering of beer. My mother was unhappy to find the way to the tree closed to us and we were sitting in the car feeling badly about how Herne would not get his beer. Suddenly there was a whooshing sound like an arrow flying through the air and then a pop. The beer went everywhere, foaming out of the can. When we looked at the can we saw that a small hole had been shot into it. We assumed Herne the Hunter had taken his beer right then and there.

As I grew older I was advised by my mother on how to use magic to solve little mundane problems but I was cautioned to never use magic carelessly. One day in school I was very naughty. We were playing bingo and I used magic to get all the numbers. I really concentrated on the numbers and won a lollipop. When I told my mother, she told me I was not supposed to use magic for trivial purposes.

*I ask Kore how she views her role as a Priestess of the Craft. Her perspective is especially interesting to me because she represents the face of a new generation of Priesthood – those who are dedicating themselves at a very young age to the most ancient vocation of all and who will be responsible for bringing the Craft forward into the next generation.*

It is important to serve the Gods, be true to my oath, and to help my brothers and sisters of the Craft. I try to live my everyday day life serving the Gods and not just in Circles. It's also important to never stop learning so that we can become more spiritual beings and thereby serve the evolution of our planet and all that is upon it. I recently saw the film "Avatar" which made all of this come home to me. We all have this connection to the planet – and not just to the planet but to everything that lives and breathes on the planet. We are all part of one organism.

There is a lot of talk lately of 2012 and what is happening with the planet. The earth has shifted on its axis at least twice in the past few years due to strong earthquakes. There are climate and weather changes around the world that are hard to ignore. The Gaia principle is very real – the earth is a living thing. People say that the human race will kill the earth. But the earth is more capable of killing the human race. If we are all connected, then the earth can dial into us as easily as we can dial into the earth. The planet has been through many ice ages. After every ice age the earth heats up again and new life forms emerge. Maybe next time a more intelligent life form will come about who will take better care of the planet.

From the perspective of moving the Alexandrian tradition forward, it is a little daunting because I don't know anyone else like me. I meet a lot of pagans my age but do not know any other Alexandrians my own age.

Doing whatever I can to help the Craft continue is something I'm very keen on, such as being a part of this book. I feel that we have a responsibility to practice, learn, teach, and represent the Craft to the very best of our abilities. Also if reincarnation is a fact then it would be nice to think that we have something to come back to.

I am still active in the Craft and am continuing my training. I have a very busy job that requires a lot of work and long hours. Still, I make sure I have every Sabbat booked off from work a year in advance. Full moons are not as easy but I try my best as I work shifts. Halloween is a must for me I book the whole week off for that. We also try to visit magical sites whenever possible. I have no plans to run a Coven in the foreseeable future. At the moment I just to try to better myself as a person, learn the Craft and try to better understand the mysteries of life.

When I think of Alex, I see him as the founder of our particular branch of Wicca, and as a very magical person who laid the groundwork for others to follow. I don't see him as a guru or someone who needs to be thought of as semi-divine, but as the man who made it possible for us to practice the Craft in the way that we do. Also as someone who was brave enough, with Maxine, to be open about being in the Craft and thereby ensuring the continued survival of Wicca, making it accessible to people who might not otherwise have found it. We as Alexandrians owe him and Maxine a great debt of gratitude for the legacy we have inherited. My mother has told me many stories about when she was in Alex and Maxine's Coven, some of them very funny, but it is what she learned there that is the basis of all the work that she, and therefore I, do in Wicca.

My mother told me a story about working with Alex and Maxine that made me laugh. She was a part of the original London Coven and there are many photographs of her with Alex which were taken during rituals that were staged for the press. In many of these photographs, an outdoor Circle was set up for the photo shoot. This Circle included a stone altar which was painted with magical symbols. Although painted to look like a huge piece of stone, this was actually a prop made out of polystyrene. At the conclusion of one of these events, my mother picked up the altar and walked away with it. A nearby reporter gasped and asked "How did you manage to pick that up?" To which my mother replied, "Magic."

When I think about the Craft today and my role in it, I am reminded of my spiritual father Chris's magical sword. I inherited the sword when he passed. I see this as a responsibility to carry on the work, for myself and for those to come, as well as honouring my Wiccan ancestors. There is both sadness and joy, sadness at loss but joy that his spirit is still with me in my spiritual work. Of course this isn't just a sword – the sword is a reminder that I need to carry on. It represents my will and forward motion. When I inherited his sword I inherited his will. When I use his sword I am an extension of his will. I know he is never really gone and I feel closer to him today than ever before. Before Chris owned the sword it was my mother's sword. And before that a Masonic sword – so it is a well used magical weapon.

Of course not all people think as I do. When you meet certain people who say things who are not Craft even though they say they are wiccan, they almost make us reject what we are. Like one time I heard "Blessed Be" used on a television show. I always believed this was something special that witches said to each other. I once saw a woman wearing a beautiful pentagram in a store and I said something nice to her thinking she was Craft. She completely shut me off and made me feel foolish. I was brought up to think a pentagram was something really special – not something to be put on as fashion. There is a real underlying mystery in our tradition that should be kept alive. We shouldn't let people take our secrets and cheapen them. We have to remember the truth and keep it safe. That's very important.

We and everything that lives is working toward the realisation that we all carry the Divine within us, that we are not separate entities but are all one. Dogma and fundamentalism are the enemies of this realisation of truth. This is what Wicca teaches me.

# All the King's Children

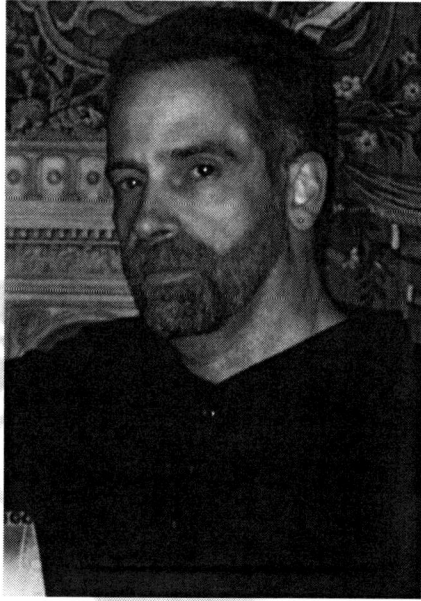

# The Plutonian Event

*Theitic*
**Third Degree High Priest**
**United States of America**

*I* was probably about three years old the night my grandmother told me about the tree. It was dark in my bedroom and a thunderstorm was rumbling around outside. I was alone in my room and frightened by the storm. My grandmother came into the room and sat on the edge of the bed. The window in my room faced north and together we could see the shadow of tree branches on the curtain. She took my hand and asked me, "Do you see that tree?" I said yes. "That tree is growing outside your window for a reason. It is watching over you while you sleep. That tree will always protect you. You can go to sleep and not worry. The tree will watch over you every night. You never have to be afraid again"

The tree outside my window was a triple-oak. I remember that I would frequently gather acorns and climb up into the place where the three trunks met. I would sit there and hold the acorns while concentrating on what I wanted my life to be like. It wasn't like wishing for something to come true. I believed it had to come true. That was how I determined what my life would be like. I got to decide what I wanted.

I loved playing with this tree throughout my childhood. The tree was my friend and, as my grandmother promised, watched over me every night.

Some years later I had a dream of an earth spirit sitting on one of the branches of the oak tree. He gave me the name Theitic – I knew the name was special and always kept it close to my heart.

When I was about thirteen, my parents sold the house and we moved to a newer one. We lived in this new home until I was a young adult. I must have been about twenty-one years old when I suddenly had this overwhelming urge to go back to the old house. I knocked on the front door and asked the new owner if I could see the tree in the backyard. The triple oak was still there – just as I remembered it. I quietly gathered some acorns and a few leaves that had fallen to the ground and put them in my pocket. A few months later the house was sold again and the new owners cut down the tree. I appreciated the special bond I had with the old oak that it would tell me to go back there one last time. It is amazing to think I have a piece of that tree in my pocket.

I was born in Providence, Rhode Island. Both of my parents are hard workers, working well into their 70's. Born of Italian descent, they have a strong sense of family. They always emphasized to me and my sister and brother that family "came first." All of my grandparents, aunts and uncles spoke Italian. It was a strong culture and not one that I could easily grow out of. Folks in many parts of the country call Rhode Island "Little Italy."My parents grew up in this same neighborhood which is as Italian as you can get.

I grew up making wine in the basement with my grandfather. I learned to cook as a kid. My grand mother taught me to bake special things at certain times of the year. At Easter she would bake bread - sometimes with a whole egg left inside to be discovered. These were for fertility. She would bake cakes shaped like chickens and rabbits. The boys would get rabbits and the girls, chickens. She would shape the same cakes into horseshoes and give one to each male head of a household. We were instructed to cover the cakes with honey before eating them to sweeten the year ahead.

My parents always pushed themselves – working in real estate, business, retail, banking, manufacturing, etc. They were not afraid to try something new. They were clever and industrious.

As a child, my life goals were to be a teacher, a magician, or a gardener. I always loved stage magic and practiced it at home, never understanding when the tricks would be replaced with "the real thing." It was easy to learn gardening. My ethnic background meant that everyone in my family had gardens – tomatoes, grapevines, mint, basil, fig trees, onions and garlic were the favorites.

My father was born and raised Catholic, and maintains a strong faith to this day. My mother was born Catholic "in name," but never practiced the religion. Having said this, it is important to know that some of the Catholic influence did spill over to the folk tradition that my mother grew up in. For example, my grandmother was not a churchgoer, but would frequently visit the local church with an empty vial to get some holy water for use at home. They also made offerings to saints in the house. I remember the Infant of Prague, St. Anne and St. Teresa in particular.

In an Italian household in the 1950's it was perfectly acceptable to be a fortune-teller and go to Catholic mass, come home from Mass and light a candle to heal a sick family member, then do the turning of the Evil Eye, and make dinner (everything started and ended with food). In my family, Catholicism was mixed with folklore. What many of my family members called prayers, today we would look at and call sorcery.

No one ever used the word strega in the context of my family. If you said this to my grandmother she would consider it an insult. If she didn't like someone or if she felt they were working magic against us, she would say they are no good or a witch. We didn't consider what she was doing as magic – like pointing the rolling pin, doing stuff with a broom – that's just what you do. I thought every home had the candles and incense burning. I grew up thinking this was what everyone did in their homes. When I got old enough to go to school and found other kids didn't do this, I couldn't believe it. "You don't use a broom to sweep people out of your house? How do you get rid of people you don't like?" "You don't have pictures of your dead ancestors in your house? Where do you put the pictures when they die?"

One of the things I do, which surprisingly I have discovered is not all that common even among witches, is that I keep an altar for my ancestors in my home. It is so important to remember that these people are still here, they may have left us in physical form but their spirits are still with us. I was asked by someone recently who my closest friends are and I listed three people. He said "I'd really like to meet them some day" to which I replied "Two of them are dead." He responded "You can't list dead people as best friends!" Who says I can't? They are still here, they are still my best friends.

When someone passes, I make a new page in a special book. I put a picture, bits of things that remind me of them, the Mass cards I get when I go to the wakes. I place candles and incense on this altar, as well as food and drink for the dead. Exactly like I was taught to do when I was a child. My older family members retained much of the folklore of Italy. My mother was born in Italy. Although there was nothing "formal" about our education of folklore, there was plenty of it around for us to learn from. Although I don't usually talk about the details, it is probably sufficient to explain that there was much use of herbs, candles, a litany of "prayers," talking to dead relatives, offerings to saints and oh, did I mention garlic?

As a child, when I visited my grandmother, she would encourage me and my siblings to watch late-night suspense and horror movies. I was always fascinated with witches or movies that focused on magic. I loved the old black and white films like Dracula and Frankenstein. My very first Halloween costume was a witch.

Because we grew up with horror films, none of us were afraid of the dark., We didn't have the fears that other kids had. If I had been told as a little boy "Don't go up to that house because an evil lady lives there,", I would have marched right up to the house and knocked on the front door. When you grow up being comfortable with the dark and with shadows, this stuff is not a problem.

I loved to watch my grandmother do the turning back of the evil eye. It seemed to stir something inside me. It wasn't until I was in my twenties before she taught me the words and showed me how to do it for myself.

My Aunt Vivian bought me my first book on magic and witchcraft when I was just fourteen years old. She passed away last year. I have a few keepsakes from her – a green glass vase, a Halloween scarf with pumpkins all over it, and three of her favorite books. The titles alone speak volumes about my unusual family – *Death Sentence, Danger Money,* and *Nursery Rhymes and Poison.* Aunt Vivian was a fun aunt!

One of my other aunts was a fortune teller. She didn't read professionally but just for family and friends. She was very good. When she passed, I was fortunate enough to get her cards.

In my family we were taught to honor the dead. Recently I was in Florida on vacation with my family. We went out to dinner one night and in the middle of dinner we picked up our glasses and toasted my grandfather's birthday. Today he would be 100 years old. I am probably a member of the only family I know who continues to have birthday parties for dead people.

My first experience in a magic Circle was a self-made rite, long before my first Initiation, performed in the woods. I was about fifteen. The rite didn't go particularly well. One should learn a bit about evocation before trying it at such a young age, unsupervised, and in the woods, no doubt. It scared the hell out of me to find that big dark noisy things lived and breathed in the woods, and could be summoned up. Of course, none of the books I had read told me how to get rid of the thing.

I conjured something I didn't understand. I took something out of a book like the Key of Solomon and read it out loud. This sort of thing was meant to be done indoors, not subject to power of the wind and other natural things. I climbed up on a rock which was jutting out of the earth. I think I had poured salt around the outside of the rock. And then I started conjuring.

It was late afternoon and the sun was going down behind me. So the area in front of me got very dark. The rock dipped down toward the East and ended in a heavily wooded area. I started to hear strange sounds coming from the woods. The hair on the back of my neck stood up and the wind started coming in strong from the East. It blew out some of my candles. I could hear these sounds coming closer to the edge of the trees. It was a low, growly, grumbling sound. It didn't go away but got louder and louder.

Then I got the feeling that whatever this was, it was coming up the rock! I didn't see anything but the air in front of me looked and felt different. At that age I had no mentors and had to go by my instincts. I remembered my grandmother yelling at the statue of a saint who had not answered her prayer. She turned the saint around and put her in the corner. She told me that sometimes you have to be very forceful to get what you want. So I picked up a stick and pointed it. I was shaking with fear but said in a strong and sure voice "I'm done with you. Go away!" I stayed on top of that rock for over an hour. The energy gradually receded and the woods were silent. I left in the opposite direction from my house and walked down the middle of the street to get home. I didn't try that again.

I first heard the name Alex Sanders in 1973; I was sixteen years old and a friend explained the differences between different types of Craft. He explained that Alexandrian was a branch of the Gardnerian Tradition. He described Alex as a magician with no bounds - a man who dared to challenge society and who went way beyond what Gerald Gardner did – Gardner was concerned about publicity but Alex wanted more and more. Like a gay person in a fabric shop, Alex couldn't get enough. I came to think of Alex as a flamboyant magician – someone who had five different kinds of wands - one for each occasion. Gardner was a more humble, folksy person.

My first Initiation into the Craft came in 1976. I was nineteen years old and living in Rhode Island. This was a family/Traditional group that sprang from the late Gwen Thompson of North Haven, CT.

I had been waiting since I was eighteen to get in and almost didn't make it. The Coven brought in an initiate just before me which brought the requisite number of witches up to thirteen, leaving no place for me. So I had to wait a few more months until a Coven hived off to get in.

I felt like Initiation was something I had done a hundred times before. It was like sitting down to eat a meal in a different place with different people around me, but it was a meal I had eaten many times before. I had been through the same experience in a different ritual in a different lifetime in a different place and time.

But the feeling of having someone perform magic on you while your third eye opens, the awareness of a magical world around you is not like any other experience. Learning that you can create your own world is overwhelming and yet familiar. You think "Oh yes, how could I have forgotten this? What buried this so deep in me that we have to uncover it again in this lifetime?"

My Initiation into the Craft moved me beyond belief. To this day, I can still see the room, smell the incense, feel the joy and see the face of my initiating High Priestess. It was an experience that I will carry in my heart and to my grave.

I was privileged to be a student of Gwen Thompson and a close friend of Elizabeth Pepper. I later took my Alexandrian Initiations and today am a Priest of four Covens in two Traditions. I also offer advice, training, and occasionally practice in a third tradition. I hope to pass along what I have learned and continue to learn to any of my students that have the ability to hear and see what was told and shown to me.

Coming into the Alexandrian Tradition for me was like tapping into something familiar, but older. I like antiques and old books. I often prefer the company of the dead over the living. The roots of things are very important to me. When I became Alexandrian I became aware of the roots of our Tradition. I asked why we didn't have a picture of Alex in our Circle. I wanted to set up a small table in the Circle with a glass of wine and his photo so he could be included in our rites.

Magically I like to tap into that river of energy that is set into motion. The river that Alex set in motion is a tumultuous place. It is not smooth. It is not something you come into and feel supported. You come into it and are tossed around. You come up for air and then go back into the rapids again. I love working with energy but my impression of Alex's energy is you either sink or swim. It's like being pushed by a coach in athletics or pushed by a dance instructor because they see your potential even when you don't. They know you can be all that you can be in the field you've chosen to work. Now if a person can create that kind of energy, it gives me a sense of what the person was like. I'm not sure if I would have liked him as a neighbor.

Alex felt as I do – "the Goddess doesn't offer social security." If you take a step on this path you must always continue to walk it. You may walk slower some days and faster others. But, there is no stopping. The Universe doesn't stop for a coffee break. If you stop, you move backwards. You can only accomplish that which you have a vision for. If you can't see it, then you can't get there.

I see my first role as a Priest as a leader. A leader of people who want to learn in order to evolve and help others evolve. I have always aspired to the words of Dion Fortune: "By the path whereon the Initiates have gone, ahead of their time, evolution is beginning to go, taking with it the race as a whole." Of course, to be a leader means that one needs to be a mentor, a teacher, a counselor, a father figure, a friend, a support system - in short, I must be what the student needs in order for the student to develop.

It is vital to me that the Craft stays alive, in whatever form it may take. I am not concerned about numbers of Initiates, just that the Craft remains alive and that the secrets of finding, raising and directing power and the wisdom of living with nature remain preserved. I hope to pass along what I have learned and continue to learn to any of my students that have the ability to hear and see what was told and shown to me.

Coming into the Craft is like tapping into pure truth – the purest truth you could ever imagine. It is the Plutonian event. Astrologers use this term to describe an event that is so remarkable, so conclusive, that it is irreversible. It is like traveling to Pluto. Once you have been to the outermost reaches of the solar system, you can't say you weren't there. There can never be a time when you weren't at Pluto.

It's also like Alice in Wonderland – once you drink the potion you can't deny the other world is there. Once you have taken the step into Initiation you can't shut it out of your life. It would be like killing a part of yourself. You can't deny that this part of yourself has been opened – doing so would be wrong and the effect of that denial would reverberate into the Universe, when you have taken a step on a spiritual path you can't go back. To think of stopping is unfathomable.

Nunhead Cemetery in South London is reputed to
be one of England's most haunted places

# The Secret Life of Stones

*Violet*
**First Degree Priestess**
**England**

*I*t all started when I was little. I had seen photographs of Maxine and Alex in magazines and newspapers while I was in primary school. I was mesmerized by what I saw – Alex looked like a magician and Maxine really looked like the Goddess. I was impressed that they were teaching witchcraft and I wished to be able to be their student. But I knew I would have to wait a long time to be old enough.

I was born and raised in Peckham, South London. I come from a family of "witchy women"- not really witches, but naturally psychic. The women in my family just knew things. It verged on ridiculousness. Obviously, something was going on, I said to my aunt once, "We are witches, aren't we?" She laughed and said "Let's just say we have our moments."

"We are all sensitive," my nan would say. I was deeply influenced by watching my "magic nan" and mum and aunt and sisters using the psychic skills that were in all of us. We made things happen, a lot of which was too much to be coincidence. This compelled me to explore my psychic abilities further. I was the only one of us that did. I knew this journey would most likely take me the rest of this lifetime and probably well into the next.

One day I saw an advertisement for the magazine series Man, Myth, and Magic and I told my aunt we had to get it. I was fascinated by the Pan -like force on the cover of the first issue, looking foreboding and exciting. It was through reading this magazine series that I got my early education in the occult on a wide range of subjects. I read about crystal skulls and witches and so much more.

I think I found out about the Atlantis Bookshop from an ad in there. This is the oldest bookshop for occult books in the world and still the best.

I wanted to know more about witchcraft and read as much as I could. I was a very advanced reader at the age of seven. I had a good collection of books myself for such a young age. I studied them thoroughly whether I understood their contents or not.

I would go into libraries with my aunt and she would let me have what I wanted on her library card. If I went on my own I would just steal the books, knowing that I was liberating them and putting them to good use. I wanted the knowledge within them no matter what. I even stole Crowley books to compare ways of magical practice. He would have loved that.

I don't know what the first book I read was, but Dion Fortune and Dennis Wheatley were among the first authors I discovered. One of my favourites was *King of the Witches*, which I thought was a very important book. I had borrowed *King of the Witches* from another kid's dad. *The Magus* fascinated me a lot and I have had three copies in my life. *Maxine Sanders, Witch Queen*, and books by Gavin & Yvonne Frost and the Farrars were in there somewhere too. I read books on every subject of the paranormal and occult including books about voodoo and demonology.

Nunhead Library in South London was the best library for occult books as they had the biggest collection. They were all kept in the "philosophy" section of the library. It was easy to take books from this library because the librarians never looked at anyone and there were no electronic security systems at that time. I just put the books under my coat. I did put books back sometimes. When I was sixteen, I borrowed *Ecstatic Mother* from a library and I really wished I had kept it as it is really rare.

Now I understand that it isn't always a good idea in a literary sense to "mix your drinks," but at the time I wanted to know everything. But I always came back to the Alexandrians. Like most children, I knew exactly what I wanted to be when I grew up. I wanted to be an Alexandrian.

My plan was to learn as much as I could about magic and then one day when I was old enough, I would meet someone who knew I was good enough to join a Coven.

I was not your average child in that I was not afraid of anything. I always believed that there was no such thing as the supernatural or paranormal. Everything was natural and normal. We just didn't understand it yet.

Nunhead Cemetery was one of my favorite places to go as a child. It is a place of peace and beauty. It was sometimes referred to as the "little brother of Highgate cemetery" due to its dodgy appearance. It was all overgrown and foreboding - a good place for all things bad to happen. There were rumours of dark forces at work there, of sinister practices and even voodoo going on there. Of course I found that very interesting.

I never feared the dead. There were a lot of deaths in the family when I was little. I was at ease with it. I helped my family prepare the dead bodies for the undertakers. We would wash and dress our dead with great care. You know when you're young and your mum says don't go out of the house with dirty underwear in case you get run over and have to go to the hospital? My aunt taught me that the dead feel the same way – they have to be clean and properly dressed before they go to the undertaker.

Throughout my adolescent years, I continued to get some exposure to the world of witchcraft around me.

When I was sixteen I was taken to visit Maxine's Coven, Temple of the Mother. (I looked older but I was too shy to talk to anyone.) I went there with a friend who needed some help.

When I was seventeen I met a couple who were good but it was the wrong time. For years I thought of them. About twelve years later I went back to see them, but they had moved. I always believed that I would meet the High Priestess again when the time was right. I met a lot of magical people over the years but was never comfortable with any so called High Priesthood that I encountered.

I felt some that I thought may be good were full of ego and seemed to attract fans rather than being serious teachers who will give serious students a chance to learn.

Meanwhile, I had been practicing on my own. I did a lot of magic, charms, hedgewitchery, potions, and divination. I had also been working with the Fellowship of Isis which includes a lot of ritual, devotional work, study, meditation, trancework and Egyptian magic. I did quite well and got by. I knew I was good – but I wanted to be great. And more than anything else, I wanted to be part of the Alexandrian lineage.

Thirty more years went by. I was a very shy person by nature and it was very difficult for me to speak with people I didn't know. Then I read that people were planning to meet for an Alex Sanders memorial service. This was in May 2008. It had been twenty years since his death.

When I arrived at the event, I saw a lot of people who knew each other. Most likely all third degree Alexandrians, I thought. The crowd didn't seem that friendly because everyone but me seemed to know someone there. Fortunately for me, there was one woman at the memorial who I had met previously at a Wiccan study group. Her name is Vivianne Crowley.

There was a ritual working. We used cord magic to bring a healthy future to the Craft and that really touched me. I really wanted to be part of this. After ritual there was a feast and I sat there thinking I have waited over thirty years for this moment. If I don't talk to someone today, that's really stupid. This is a golden opportunity.

Vivianne, as if she could read my mind, came up to me and asked me how I was. I opened up to her and told her how I felt at that moment – that I desperately wanted to find an Alexandrian Coven and I want to be part of this future everyone is speaking of. She said "Leave it to me," and went off. A little later she took me by the hand and said "There is someone I want you to meet." She introduced me to Scott, the man who would become my teacher.

Scott was one guy who really stood out in the crowd. I had seen him across the room earlier in the day; I thought he really looks the business.

Scott seemed like the kind of guy who knows what he's doing. He has fabulous eyes and a great aura. I had an idea in my mind of what kind of High Priest I wanted to join up with, and he was it. Someone who is serious and strict, but with whom you are comfortable enough to talk to. He has the right amount of fear to get it done. I think it is important to fear sometimes. If someone is nice to you all the time it's not good. You have to think oh no, I've got to get this right or he's going to go mad.

I wanted a serious minded teacher so I kind of tested him. I thought I would say something fluffy and see how he reacted. I don't remember what I said but it was really fluffy and he gave me a look that said are you serious or what? And I thought, that's the look I wanted. It was important for me to learn from someone who would give me a chance – someone who would say "OK, you want to learn? Here's a chance - get on with it." Some of the people I met in the past would initiate only those who "sucked up" to them or who were part of the "in crowd." I'm not an "in crowd" person, so this was great. I was so excited. A few months of pre-Initiation training followed that meeting and I finally became an Alexandrian Priestess. I got on from there and it's been a very happy journey.

I had been training with Scott for a while when I attended an incense workshop he was teaching. While talking with him, I found out that the High Priestess who I knew I would meet again was his teacher for second and third degrees. I was surprised. As it turns out, I was right. I would see her again when the time was right. My journey had gone full Circle - I had to wait until she initiated my teacher and then he came back for me.

Scott taught me that you have to be a Priestess of the Craft 24/7 and not just in Circle. I am always helping people. I work in a hospital and help people all day. I also run a resident's association in my neighborhood that offers support to those members of the community in need. I believe it is important to teach people how to put good out into the universe. The world would be a much better place to be if we each try to make a difference. Some people say there is so much bad in the world that we should just be selfish. Grab what you can. I can't think like that. I believe in karma and reaping the benefits of karma. I had a lot of bad luck in my life and now it is turning round. Inside my Coven I want to learn as much as I can and support my brothers and sisters of the Craft as best as I can. But outside the Coven, my work as a Priestess must go on.

I hope to have a Coven of my own some day. I'm not taking this for granted though. Like in a relationship, people meet and then plan out the rest of their lives all at once. They think, we're going out now, then we'll get engaged, then we'll get married. I'm not thinking like that. When I get over-confident I usually fall on my ass. It is important to learn patience. Now I just hope to attain the next degrees before I'm 50.

My perception of Alex has deepened since my Initiation into the Alexandrian tradition. I feel he has done a lot of things right and some wrong. People admire him and criticize him. There is a difference between a good man and a great man. Alex was a great man. When I look back at how I was first impressed by him in those photographs, I realize he had power. The power he had was partly glamouring. He was very knowledgeable and through his personal experience started something wonderful. We really need to carry this on.

When I was growing up, I spent a lot of time in my aunt's garden. This is where my magical journey began. The garden was very large and overgrown. It was my favourite place to be. I could feel the magic there. I used to hide under the rhubarb and lay my head on the rockery so I could hear the stones breathe. When people think of a garden being alive they think of flowers and plants and insects of course. But there is so much more to discover in a garden. There is a secret life that is only revealed when you are very still and listen very carefully. Everything is alive around you – not just the green growing things, but everything. To be alone in the quiet beauty of this magic place attuned me. As a child, I could not imagine what wonders lay ahead of me. But I did know with all my heart that none would be greater than listening to the stones breathe.

I believe that what we have inside us the most important thing to carry us forward. You can't lie about who you are – either to yourself or to anyone else. I've heard it said that it is not the destination, but the journey. Sometimes the journey covers a great distance. Sometimes there is a reason things take time. I could look back at the decades it took me to get this far and think why did it take me so long to get to where I am today? But it doesn't matter. I have decades ahead of me. I have to make the most of it and do my best.

# Climbing the Rose


*Dean*
**Second Degree High Priest**
**Australia**

*To each of us comes a moment in which everything changes. Whether we realise it at the time or whether this awareness arrives by retrospect may vary. But the fact that nothing can ever be quite the same afterward is indisputable. For some of us this moment comes quietly like a whisper of words long forgotten. But for others the moment arrives with wings and with talons.*

I was 17years old when a very important event occurred that changed my life forever.

I was working as a waiter in a small restaurant in Christchurch City, New Zealand – Tony's Steak House. It was Friday afternoon. The city was busy, full of smog, and stifling hot. I was on my way to work when I was stopped by a street beggar, asking for some money and a cigarette. He was a tall man dressed in ragged clothing. I felt badly for him, so I gave him $10.00 and all my cigarettes except one, which I kept for smoke break. As I turned away he grabbed my arm, stared into my eyes and said "You will face death tonight, but fear not, you will be saved." I thought that he was insane and headed off to work.

The night was incredibly busy at the restaurant and we were short staffed, both in the kitchen and on the floor. It was the worst night possible to be working there. After work, four of us decided to climb into a car and head off for a night picnic around Monks Bay.

I passed out in the car and before you know it, I was facing a female Maori Elder (with full Ta Moko on her chin), instructing me to go back. I was quite taken aback by this, shocked and unsure of where I was. Then I suddenly woke up in Southern Cross Hospital. I started to get off my bed and three nurses came running to advise me that I had been in a serious car accident. Then the pain came rushing in and I passed out again. The Maori woman reappeared and said that I need to take my place with the Brotherhood to help with the Great Work. I had no idea what all of this meant and I really thought that I was losing the plot.

The next day I woke up in intense pain (it was my 18th birthday) and was told that I had a fractured skull, a broken arm and a broken leg, with major damage to my left eye. All I could think was that I needed to pee and that I was in so much pain. I did not understand the visions I had experienced. In retrospect, I realise these were my very first steps into my spiritual development. I had no idea what I was in for.

After six weeks of intensive care I was finally healed enough to leave the hospital. Eventually I had the plaster removed and was back at work. I had forgotten about all of the visions because I thought that it was just a dream and nothing more. Three years went by and I had developed a drug/alcohol induced psychosis, followed by major depression. No one knew what was going on with me or how to help me.

*Dean's vision of the Maori elder on the night of the car crash turned out to be more than a pain and hysteria induced dream. Perhaps forgotten on all but a cellular level, Dean had been born into a Maori tribe. A series of unfortunate events caused him to be taken away from his mother at two years of age and sent to live with his European grandparents.*

My mother was jailed in Brisbane for trafficking narcotics when I was two years of age. She later turned her life around and graduated with her nursing degree while in prison and I am very proud of her achievements. She is a constant reminder that we all make mistakes but are not beyond redemption.

I was mostly unhappy during my childhood. I could not concentrate at school. In fact I had to stay behind a year due to learning difficulties. My Maori teacher said it was the European education system that I had difficulty with, not the ability to learn. Studies have shown that most Polynesian children intake learning vastly different from European children.

I continued to call for my mother. I would wake in the middle of the night crying - feeling lost and abandoned. I became quite ill, suffered from continuous ear infections and an undiagnosed depression that became a huge problem. I would have been happy to stay with my grandparents forever but eventually my father sent for me and I went to live with him and his new wife. They thought that it would be beneficial for me to go see a family counselor. I remember she tried to hypnotise me and became frustrated when it wouldn't work.

My father loved three things in life – soccer, the Beatles and surfing. He was a bit of a hippie in his youth and really enjoyed outdoor adventures. He worked as a carpenter building houses and one of my favourite memories is sitting on his lap sipping the froth off his first beer of the night. We had a large family - five sisters and one brother. I love them very much.

As a child I never had an overt interest in the occult. There were however, a few strange encounters. One particular incident happened when I was about three years old and living with my English grandparents. My grandmother saw me playing and talking to someone who was not in the room. Apparently this occurred several times in my early childhood but I don't recall any of this at all. The next encounter was when I was seven years old. I saw an old woman's face in the dark moon at home – I screamed. It freaked me out. It may have been an eclipse; I don't know. But the vision was frightening. Another event was when I was nine years old and the vacuum cleaner moved by itself. It danced like a snake and hissed at me, I was petrified. There was a friend of the family named Jackie and she came running to comfort me.

Much later on in my life, I went with my family to one of the Nambassa three day music, crafts and alternative lifestyles festivals held in New Zealand. I met a Lakota Indian man who stayed in a Tipi with his wife and children. His wife performed a magical smoking ceremony for us. It was beautiful. They had stage healers who asked people from the audience to come forward. I watched a Shaman cleanse and heal another man. It was the most incredible thing that I had experienced.

I remember going up on the stage and asking him to heal me. He said "But there's nothing wrong with you!" I didn't care; I just wanted to be there and to feel that power.

My parents were not very religious people. They were just your average folk who grew veggie crops, and raised a few farm animals. We had chickens and a goat who ate all of our grass, clothes, and anything that she could get a hold of. We always had fresh cottage cheese, fruit from our own trees and fresh eggs. Dad would pop down to the beach and catch the odd fish or two and we went out and collected shellfish most Sundays. I loved my childhood very much, but I yearned terribly for my birth mother.

I do remember one event that occurred in church. I performed in a church concert which re-enacted the death of Jesus Christ. The concert ended suddenly when one of the "disciples" in the play broke his arm on stage. I was eight years old at the time and pretty freaked out about the entire incident, so I never went back. Christianity just did not do it for me after that.

I guess my first stage of training in the occult began after the accident that nearly killed me. I had lost my job and my flat and had arrived home on a dark and stormy night to ask my family for help. They welcomed me home again in the way that only a family can, to help me to get well.

Shortly afterward I met a lady called Linda. I called her a gypsy, but in actuality she was very into Native American spirituality. She introduced me to the world of cartomancy, meditation, crystal healing and trance. I was given books to read like *Medicine Woman* by Lynn Andrews, *Medicine Wheel* by Sun Bear/Wabun and the *Don Juan Teachings* by Carlos

Castaneda. I began my moccasin walk, which is an earth walk. This was when I learned how to study my environment - the wildlife, the sun and the seasons, the moon and the tides. This was a magical time for me and it was the most beautiful training that I ever received.

I began to learn how to honour and respect nature, its beauty and its dangers. Gifts of thanks were placed at certain areas when I was collecting material and by doing so I developed a practice of communication with my environment. I made my first rattle, medicine pouch, smudging stick and peace pipe. These were the very first tools that I used to perform magic to communicate with spirits from other dimensions. I practiced all of these ceremonies on my own and I was always skyclad. This was a beautiful time, but then a voice in the dark came and gave me a gentle nudge to move on. It was time, and so I did.

*Some may consider it ironic that Dean was born into an indigenous native tradition and yet discovered his spirituality in the teachings of the Native American ways. However these first steps into a spiritual way of life would lead him back to his own people. Such is the way of magic, or as a dear friend once put it so eloquently – "power finds its way."*

*Dean saw an advertisement in the paper asking for volunteers to help the Maori people. Like many indigenous tribes, they were experiencing problems within their community including poverty and unemployment. Dean felt he could help and volunteered to help in whatever way he could. At the time he didn't realise that his selfless act of kindness to help those in need would bring him back to his tribe. Recognising him immediately as one of their own, he was taken in by a Maori family and lived with them for many years.*

I found myself on a Marae (Maori Village) where I undertook the next stage in my spiritual journey. Here I was blessed and initiated back into my Tribe, Ngati Paoa – Tainui. These were the same people I was separated from when I was a baby.

The elders treated me with love, kindness and respect, but above all a firm lesson was given that spirituality begins on the end of a spade. It was with our hands that we blessed Mother Earth. The elders of my tribe were 70 or 80 years of age – perhaps older. Yet they worked just as hard as the young folk did. We all worked very long hours together, ate our meals together, went hunting together, danced, and sang songs together.

At the end of the day we would fall asleep together. I felt accepted as a family member within my tribe. I learned the art of weaving baskets, dancing skirts and mats – all made from natural fibre called Harakeke (New Zealand flax). I was taught how to be hospitable to guests through the art of Powhiri, which is a Maori Welcoming Ceremony.

Because we were living in such close contact with each other, there were moments when arguments would flare up. But they were resolved quickly so we all could move on peacefully.

I had a very good teacher during this period of my life. She was a Maori Elder (Mata kite) and a Medicine Woman. She had a young face for her age, but very old dark brown eyes, and long black hair that reached down to her waist. Most importantly, she had full use of her third eye – she was born with this gift. We called her Nanna and she taught me how to commune with my Great Grandmother. This may have been my first exposure to Goddess worship.

I lived in this magical world for many years and became extremely wealthy in knowledge and spirituality. Unfortunately we were very poor financially. We lived on bread, water, and what crops we could grow. That's what it was about. My elders taught me that spirituality begins not in a book but through action. If you are hungry you better start ploughing the ground and planting potatoes. If you want meat for dinner, you will have to kill a chicken and cook it yourself.

I remember we had about twenty-five chickens which were used to feed the tribe. I can still see them with heads removed, hanging by clothesline so the blood could drain out. It is so much easier today - I just pull out my credit card and away I go.

After many years living with the Maori, I felt it was time for me to move on again. I left because I needed my independence and I knew there was more for me to discover – that on the horizon was another learning curve in my spiritual development I needed to experience.

So I moved and found a flat in the big city, and went back to working as a waiter in one of the local hotels.

One of the first things I noticed about city life was the difference in the taste of the water. Here they drank town water – it was horrible. They put fluoride in their water and treated it with chemicals. I suppose those who grow up with this water adapt to it but I could taste it all. If you've ever had fresh rainwater you will understand how sweet it is – it's pure – that's the stuff we really need to use in our circles.

In addition to my work in the hotel I also had a part time job working as a cabaret artist, lip synching to 70's rock music completely dressed as a drag queen. The popular film *Priscilla Queen of the Desert* had just come out and suddenly there were men in frocks everywhere. That was hilarious and I had a lot of fun. But as the old saying goes, all good things must come to an end. Still sensing the need to move onward, I left the shores of Christchurch and headed off to the Great Southern Lands of Australia in search of new adventure.

Truth is I was very lonely and wanted to know what love was about – I was still quite angry at the world because of everything that had happened to me. So I went back into prayer to the Great Grandmother and asked how can I know what love is if I don't have anyone to share my life? I didn't want any ordinary Joe Bloke. I wanted to meet someone very special. I had no way of knowing what the Gods had in store for me.

It was January 2000, Sydney to be precise. I was out on the town with friends when I suddenly decided to head home early. I had been feeling very lonely and down for quite some time.

Yes I had friends, but there was never that special someone, just for me. It was hot and the humidity was intense so I decided to go for an evening swim at one of the small beaches. I stripped off all my clothes and was about to go in the water when I looked up at the sky and there was a bright red moon just hovering above the city of Sydney. It was huge and I felt mesmerized by its size. I walked into the water up to my waist. The sea was calm, tempered warm, and peaceful. Then I felt something brush past me. It was a shark. I was quite startled by its presence but it quickly swam away. I looked up at the moon again and felt the urge to scream and run out of the water. But for some strange reason I was compelled to stay. Naked and feeling vulnerable, I raised my arms up to the sky facing the blood red moon. All of a sudden I felt an enormous energy flowing through me and out of my mouth came these strange words, "Oh great grandmother, sister, mighty daughter of old, ancient one, I call to you...." I stood for while longer in the water and was quite stunned by what I had just done. Then I realised that people could be watching me and feeling self conscious of this I left in quite a hurry. When I got dressed I turned to face the moon and blew a kiss. This was the first time I worshipped the Goddess.

A month later, I went to one of the Sydney bars and there I met a wonderful man named Stuart.

I was quite taken aback by him at first, but then as we talked I felt like a school kid after getting a first kiss. We left the bar together and just by coincidence we were catching the same boat to Manly. Later I would learn that he was staying on the same road on which I lived. I scratched my head with all of these bizarre coincidences. Then I remembered my prayer to the Goddess on the night of the red moon. "Surely not", I said to myself, "things like this don't happen to me, I am nothing special just your ordinary kind of guy". Then I thought to myself, "I must have summoned him, but how?" I was very puzzled by this and started to remember the journey of *Medicine Woman* and *Don Juan*. I then realised that strange things like this do happen.

That night I couldn't sleep, I was constantly thinking about him and the strange circumstances by which we met. We decided to go out again and went out to dinner at one of the local seafood restaurants. He was very easy to talk with and we started to really get to know one another. We were both very nervous about talking of our spirituality but eventually he told me that he was a Wiccan High Priest. I was moved to hear this and knew it had to be the Goddess who brought us together. I took his hand in mine and said that my prayers had been answered. I've been looking for you for a very long time, I told him. I didn't want to admit it, but I knew that I was in love.

Stuart told me he was an Alexandrian High Priest. I was vaguely aware of Alex and Maxine Sanders. In my early childhood they popped up in the papers once or twice, but I was too young to remember the fine details. I asked Stuart to teach me the ways of Alexandrian Witchcraft and happily he agreed, but he made it abundantly clear that the teachings are strictly female to male and that everything flows through the Matriarch because she is the Spiritual Advisor.

I had my first experience in the magic circle in the year 2000 under the watchful eyes of the Alexandrian Initiates. The circle was cast by a young first degree initiate and it was marvelous. This was a beautiful experience and I felt loved, protected and respected. The experience that frightened me the most was when I conjured my first circle and it worked. I couldn't believe myself. It was like a drug, I wanted more. I got greedy and found myself practicing how to cast a circle regularly.

During this time I attended an Esbat with other Alexandrian Initiates. The purpose of the gathering was to perform magic for a healing (cord magic to be precise) and I was thrown in the deep end with no training or warning, just instructed to get to the work at hand and so I did. Some of the other initiates did not appreciate my presence because I was not initiated at that stage. As a result political issues arose between some of the other coven members because of my attendance as a non-initiate. My presence did not seem to hinder the spell. The spell was successful and I was happy to have helped.

The training for my first degree initiation was intense. I had to demonstrate in front of a panel of Alexandrian Initiates that I could cast a circle and hold the boundary on my own. In addition to this I also had to demonstrate that I could work magic, embody the God, respect the High Priesthood by following through with the training requirements and above all be completely trustworthy. The training that I received was thorough and very strict, and required a very high level of discipline from the student. This training can last up to a year and a day and then a decision is made whether or not the postulant is initiated.

I was initiated into the craft in April 2001. I remember my initiation very well. It was one of the most incredible experiences I had ever had in my life. A week before the initiation I was called out to the Elder's farm for dinner. They had decided that I was a suitable candidate to be initiated into the Craft. I was to go on a strict diet where I was not allowed to consume certain things. One of them was no caffeine for six days and six nights. (I found out later I was only meant to be on this crazy diet for three days, not six) I had to meditate several times daily. I was instructed to have cold ritual showers regularly. During this time my body was going through all sorts of withdrawal symptoms, so I began to weave a hand basket to occupy my trembling hands and mind during my spare time.

Unfortunately for me, due to financial issues, I had to work. At that time I worked as a waiter at a café in a small town. Oh my Gods, can you just imagine it, here I am making coffee for everyone and I was not allowed one sip. That was the worst test that I had to undergo. Everyone has weaknesses, mine was coffee and I only needed one cup in the morning. So you can figure out what sort of state I was in – a mess.

On the day in question, I unfortunately did not have the choice to have the day off work to prepare myself. I was at the café, it was about 11am in the morning when a man sitting at a table, closed his eyes, leaned forward and died. I watched people frantically performing CPR but then I looked up and saw his spirit rise from his body, I knew he was gone. The ambulance arrived and took the man away. Conn, one of the Greek workers, called to me and said, "Dean, don't say anything, no one will understand. Come with me to the cellar and help me with the vegetables" and so I did. We worked together in silence, then I burst into tears. Conn patted me on the back and said that "it will be alright." I was in a right mess withdrawn from being on a crazy diet and now a man dying at our café, my emotions were all over the place.

Finally the night came and a High Priestess from another coven came and picked me up. She didn't speak to me – not a word. We drove for miles and then suddenly the car came to a halt. I was dropped at the gate and told to walk to the house. It was dark, freezing cold and the wind was howling as I approached the little house at the farm. I knocked on the door several times and waited, no one came. I knocked again, and then suddenly a grumpy old man dressed in black opened the door. He grabbed me sternly and instructed me to enter, place the objects that I was told to bring on the table, prepare myself and wait in the spare room. I did as I was told. I was frightened, starving, cold and all alone; I felt like an abandoned child that no one cared for. My mind was experiencing all sorts of strange things to the point that I actually thought that I was going insane. I could hear strange sounds coming from a distance as I sat behind the closed door. Then suddenly, the door burst opened and a tall man stood glaring at me and spoke to me. I was petrified, but a voice in the back of my mind said, it will be ok, so I continued forth.

I knew from this point on there was no turning back; all I could do was take a deep breath, follow instructions and continue on. It was an incredible experience; the suspense of curiosity was overwhelming. Suddenly I was taken into a room full of strange smells and sounds, my heart was pounding rapidly, the sensation was astounding. I went blank. I left my body and experienced a journey to the outer realms, the home of the Mighty One. This was a place that I had been to before in my early years on my Moccasin journey. I returned to my body with the stranger looking at me to see if I was okay, suddenly there were all these people around me, they were worried about my wellbeing. I heard another person say, "He's gone man", and then I started to come around, followed by another voice calling me to respond to a series of words. I vaguely remember what I was asked to do, then I muttered a reply, "Yes", I think I said. It was the most incredible experience I had been through. After the Initiation I felt like I was at a Roman banquet. But, I really didn't understand what had happened, my body was vibrating all over, I was still in a daze from the experience. It was wonderful, unusual, scary, then warm, but at the same time very lonely and cold. It was like I was on a natural high, almost euphoric. I was taken home and then I passed out early due to exhaustion.

As amazing as my initiation was, in reality it almost didn't happen. Just prior to my initiation I had received an unexpected phone call from the elders. I was summoned to a meeting to respond to a complaint that someone had made against me. A group of Alexandrian Initiates from elsewhere in Australia had put together a poorly investigated theory, based on kitchen gossip. I was accused of being disrespectful to the High Priesthood, and my sexuality was put on display. I was surprised to learn that in the Australian Alexandrian line many witches believed that homosexuals were not considered suitable for initiation. As far as I know Stuart had been the first gay man brought into the line and this was a problem for some of the witches. However, what they didn't know was that I was being trained and initiated by the Matriarch. As per the tradition that was handed down, the representative of the Goddess made absolutely sure that I was indeed properly prepared.

My initiators, quite rightly, queried and investigated this complaint. My tutors were questioned about my training and coven etiquette. The elders asked everyone if I had ever done anything against the Craft, Wicca, or the Alexandrian tradition.

The answer was "no". So my initiators said they found me more than a suitable candidate for the craft and that personal issues should be kept out of the decision about one's worthiness to be initiated. As for the concerns about my sexuality, the High Priestess said that who I choose to love has nothing to do with whether or not I am suitable for the priesthood. I had never been subjected to so much humiliation ever in my life before. The whole thing was extremely embarrassing and I felt that my honour and dignity as man had been betrayed. It is difficult for me to understand this type of prejudice and sometimes I can't wait to get to heaven and talk to our craft elders over a good cup of tea and ask what were you thinking?

In searching for the truth of who was involved in discrediting my good name, I sadly learned that the rumour came from the priestesses I trusted within my very own coven. Valuable friendships were damaged and many people were badly hurt from this extraordinary event. In fact, when the truth finally came out, it destroyed our entire coven. Ironically I was accused of causing all the issues. I was held responsible for everyone's departure and the collapse of our precious coven. This had an enormous effect on me for many months afterward and taught me a lot about perfect love and perfect trust.

I did eventually receive sincere apologies from those that were involved much later on down the line. Unfortunately it was far too late, the damage was already done. During this time I had to find another way to worship our Gods without relying on anyone but myself and this made me much stronger. I am much happier now and I feel that I have grown to be better initiate because of it. This part of my story reminds me what a High Priestess once said to me many years ago, "are you prepared to suffer in order to learn?" Unaware of the consequences, I foolishly said yes.

Afterward one of the elders said to me that some of the other initiates might have been frightened of me because of my tribal background. My ancestors know a lot about death, the world of spirits, the rites of passage. When a Maori gets older there is a whole pile of work done to prepare them for the afterlife and help them bridge the gap between the world of the living and the world of the dead. There are specific protocols that must be adhered to and that they only call upon the spirit world when it is absolutely necessary. The ancestors might be busy learning something new in the afterlife and we could be interrupting them, which is not good. The spirits of the dead will then reach out to you when they can talk, but it can be any time of the night or day and you must be ready. This sort of thinking frightens people who do not understand.

We all spend a lot of energy and time on life and all the rest of it. But when the subject of death came up I would ask questions like where do all the witches' bodies go when we die? Everyone scratched their heads and said they are buried in the grave sites provided of course. You've got to be joking, I responded, after living our life as a witch our bodies are taken and placed in consecrated Christian ground? I suggested we work together within our tradition to get some land through the Government to bury our dead. This is something we are still working toward but there have been some setbacks.

Today I view the role of a High Priest to be the representative of the Horned God, to honour and serve the representative of the Goddess, the High Priestess. We are responsible for the Earth Magic and balance the Gods through worship and ritual. We are also living representatives of the God as the comforter and consoler. As such we are there to facilitate wisdom to our brothers and sisters in times of need.

In some situations, the High Priest can also be seen as the Man in Black who is seldom seen and rarely attends coven rituals. In this role he has the capacity to go between covens disseminating information and sometimes summoning initiates to attend important meetings or gatherings. They can also operate between other craft systems as mediators, such as settling disputes or investigating problematic situations. But above all, the High Priests are responsible for protecting the craft and the coven from life threatening situations. We are expected to stand on the front line and speak for the initiates if necessary and to keep secret the sacred acts of all

Temple Rites. It is my understanding that we are responsible for banishing our oppressors should they attempt to do us harm.

If there is media involvement, the High Priest usually will step forward and speak on behalf of the Craft – not the High Priestess. She is the Spiritual Advisor of the Craft. It is my understanding that the High Priests are the external Managers of the Craft; whereas the High Priestess is the internal Manager of the Coven.

I feel it is very important to perpetuate the craft for future generations; but the question is how? I consider that I have an active role in participating in this but to what end? All I can think of right now is that I would like to honour my elders who have dedicated their lives to the Craft and pass their wisdom over to those who are worthy.

I come from a dedicated system that is mainly focused on the development of the Priesthood. The male role in the Craft is just as vital as the female role and it is important that these roles are conjoined to bring balance and blessedness. I have had difficulty in believing in the one powerful God or the one Goddess concept; I am not convinced that any deity is the supreme God Head. I feel they both, in turn, have their day or night of glory.

I honour and worship the Great Mother, and the Mighty One who grants her power to do 'The Great Work'. I see the potential of the Priesthood in the Craft operating in a balanced way for everyone to love and enjoy. I feel that shared power and shared responsibilities between men and women, High Priest and High Priestess, is the proper way to run the craft.

Six months after my initiation, I got the shock of my life when I went to conjure the circle and was told that was the priestess' role. The next shock was when I went to cast a spell during an Esbat. Once again, I was told that I could not do this because the priestess is the representative of the Goddess, therefore she must cast all spells. Well, this was no fun for me. Here I am with all of my spiritual training and expertise and am now being told that I basically must surrender all my power to the priestess for her to do it all. This has never sat comfortably with me but in order to learn, I did as I was instructed to do.

I have developed a great understanding from my Craft training and I now see a need for additional work to be included. I am working on a different approach of worship. I am practicing and experimenting with magic on many different levels, documenting and assessing each method that I discover. I see the craft as a constantly evolving system that continually needs feeding in order for it to improve. This is practiced by trial and error.

It is very important for me to bring forward something that focuses on individual training needs. The system that I come from is extremely challenging and I realize that the Craft is simply not for everyone. Far too many people who have come from our system simply couldn't cope with the work and the endless training requirements. This is something that I have discovered to be worldwide and not just in Australia. Dedication to the Craft by practice is my priority now.

The Craft that I would like to see in the future is one where the power and responsibility are balanced between men and women. The Craft is my passion, my love, my pleasure and my joy. It takes priority in my life and is as important to me as work, home and family commitments I am determined to do whatever I can to keep the tradition alive.

I have heard that Alex Sanders was an extraordinary man who had special qualities and I would like to think that he helped people with all of his knowledge and spiritual techniques. I look at him as a head father figure for the Craft, who supported Simon Goodman to bring the Alexandrian tradition to Australia. This is something for which I am extremely grateful.

Alex explored different levels of consciousness. From my perspective, he was a man looking for spiritual wisdom; but was perhaps a bit blinded to the price other people close to his heart would have to pay for his development into the occult.

From what I have read about Alex, I think that he was a gifted and talented man who wanted to bring a particular system of craft into the occult world. He tested boundaries and explored many avenues of magic to make this happen. Alex opened up a doorway into another spiritual world for many people. Contrary to belief, I'd like to think that Alex Sanders re-awakened Witchcraft and put it back on track in its rightful place. May the "King of the Witches" rest in peace – Blessed Be.

One of the most significant magical experiences in my life started the day I received an unexpected call from a High Priestess, asking if I would be interested in attending the annual pagan Beltaine festival and being the representative of the Horned God in the ritual. I was thrilled and said that I would get back to her as soon as I could. I hung up the phone and my heart was pounding, I couldn't believe that I was being asked to do this. I called my Elders and asked if I could have their blessing to go and I was instructed to come out and talk to them about this before making a final decision. That night Stuart and I drove out to the farm where the

Elders were living. We sat down, ate dinner, and drank a lot of wine. We talked for hours about the dogs, the horses, and the weather. But the subject of the Beltaine festival never came up. Frustrated, I burst out with the very question, 'Well am I allowed to go to the festival or what?" The High Priestess gave me one of those frumpy frowns and in a low voice replied, "Yes you can go, with our blessing."

It was the Friday before the main event and I was in one of those stressed out moods; Stuart and I eagerly packed everything up in our little red car and headed on the seven and a half hour drive from our home. I was nervous as all hell. It had been quite some time since I had seen most of these initiates. Remember that these were the very people who protested about my initiation into the Craft and I had to face them all again. I felt I had an opportunity to demonstrate in front of everyone that my initiation was valid and that I was a worthy priest of the Craft.

We finally arrived and we were invited to stay at the leader's campsite, which is something that I had never done before. I was just bursting at the seams and desperately wanted to get the whole event over and done with and then go home. There were many people there that I had not met before.

We set up camp, still feeling very anxious and insecure about the whole thing. I felt it would help if I had a little wine to settle my nerves. We made some small talk and I soon went to bed in one of the Caravan trucks. I had a terrible night's sleep. It was a very cold, uncomfortable, and I had a million things running through my head about the ritual. Finally, just as I managed to go to sleep, the birds started chirping with their morning call.

I got up, lit the campfire, made coffee and had a small breakfast. The remainder of the day was spent fasting, except for a small amount of water. The festival site was in the crater of a dormant volcano. I went for a walk up to the summit of the crater. It was beautiful and that gave me some peace of mind. Upon my return we had a quick run through of the ritual and I started to panic a bit. I was exhausted from the night before and had a thumping headache. So I decided to lie down for an afternoon nap. I went out like a light apparently, and was snoring my head off.

The remainder of the day went by quickly and before you know it, the bonfire had been prepared and people had started to gather near the centre of the ritual area all dressed in different coloured robes. I was kept hidden in the truck. I tried to do a centering meditation to settle myself down, but that didn't work. Outrageously nervous, I eventually got my act together enough to prepare for the ritual. My face was painted black and my body painted with stripes of dark marks. I was barefoot, and dressed in a brown loin cloth. I wore a horned crown and was wrapped in a cloak.

I was instructed to go around the edge of the circle and to jump on top of a large boulder at the appropriate moment.

Everyone gathered around the unlit balefire and the Circle was cast. I could hear the calling of the Watchtowers. I knew it was my turn soon and moved closer to the boulder, with the hope that no one would see me. I stood behind an old oak tree and began to call quietly to the Ancient One, "Oh great Mighty One, Horned God, Cernunnos, Lord of Light, Lord of Power, Lord of the Hunt, descend upon thy priest and servant…" He didn't come at first. I felt frustrated. I was petrified of the thought that I would not be able to perform the rite properly and bring the God through for everyone. I had major heart palpitations occurring, as I could feel the banging of the drums.

Then the summoning began and I knew that I had to be on top of the boulder at a precise time. I ran from behind the tree, discarded the cloak and jumped up high onto the boulder. There was a roar from the crowd of people. I felt the Horned One enter my body and looked down through his eyes. I felt large, strong, and sexually hungry. I jumped down and ran towards the unlit bonfire that was circled with maidens. The drums began to beat; dust swirled up into the air as I pounded forward. Then the girls in pretty dresses surrounding the unlit balefire began to scream as I circled around them. Huge shrieks of excitement surrounded the circle as the chase began. The girls ran as though they were fleeing for their lives. The energy pulled me closer to the centre; and around and around I went. I could see the young virgin huntress ducking in between the other girls trying to get away from me. I finally caught her and a voice called out, "He's got her!" The Horned God had arrived.

There she was, the young Goddess - beauty, divine, fertile and pungent with sensuality. We came together at the altar, kissed passionately, and parted from one another. The crowd roared. I crowned her with flowers and we lit the balefire together. The witches performed the spiral dance. The maiden returned to the crowd and I vanished back to the cabin. The ritual continued with dancing and chanting, and as I looked back I could see an image of a male and female spirit swirl up above the flames of the Balefire. I knew that I had done well and that the Gods were present. I was very happy.

I cleaned myself off and approached the leaders, thanking them for letting me partake in this amazing ritual. They were speechless. I was later congratulated by many elders of the craft for what they considered to be a wonderful ritual. I looked back over the years at all the different teachings that I had gone through to get to this point in my life; and how grateful I am for having such brilliant people in my life to learn from – what a wonderful experience.

I've tried to recreate this experience at different points in my life but it is never the same. That's the way of magic – you can say the same words in the same place and do the same things and nothing ever happens the same way twice.

Everyone needs something to drive them forward. And holding the memory of this event in my heart – when the God answered my prayer on that Beltaine night – motivates me to keep moving forward.

Sometimes when you are dealing with people things can get quite complicated, especially when people tend to bring their personal lives into the Craft. Looking back on my own experiences, I can honestly say that the first degree initiation tends to bring the worst out in a person. I was fortunate enough to receive a warning about this from my initiator. My High Priestess gave me sound advice when she told me to look within and search out any ugly skeletons in my closet and deal with them before undertaking initiation. This is something that I am still working on today. My advice to those who seek initiation is to remain focused on the communion and worship of the Old Gods, the initiations will follow later on when the time is right.

There have been many obstacles that have encouraged me to close the door and stop working the Craft. But for some strange reason, I seem to keep coming back for more. In the past I have thrown my hands up in the air and told the Gods to leave me in peace, but they don't. Sooner or later they tap me on the shoulder, provide me with some strength to get back on the horse, and keep striving forward. I think that if you have a great love for magic, like I do, you get better at shrugging off old debris or unwanted issues as they can often weigh you down or stop you from progressing.

As one High Priestess said to me, it is very important for everyone to remain focused on their personal demons and not allow these demons to hinder other people. Blaming other people or pointing out other people's shortcomings, stops our own spiritual growth. Forgiveness and letting go is a lifetime project of mine.

Once an initiation is done, it can never be undone. Once you give yourself over and go through that rite of passage, you can never go back. This is why the elders are really strict. I was taught that initiation is not like tying your shoelace. If you tie your shoelace you can always undo it. Initiation is like cutting the lace. Once cut, those threads never go back together. This is not to be taken lightly and you must put some thought into this. By asking for initiation you are asking to be part of the Great Goddess and Horned God and to do their work for rest of your life. This is not "here today, gone tomorrow." You really have to think about it.

Remember too that you will be tested. People will test you. The Gods will test you. Be prepared for both. I was not prepared for people to test me. But they did. They tested me with their energy and their ego. Then the Gods have their go at you. It's a double whammy but you can't do without it.

If you are walking the path of the Goddess it is not all little butterflies flitting around, beautiful flowers, and little bunnies. There is death and blood and guts involved. There is sweat, tears, and pain. If you think the Craft is all soft billowing clouds, you are not suitable. The Horned God is terrifying and delivers some serious truths. He is Lord of Death as well as Life. The Lady is not only Virgin, She is Mother and Hag too. This is not like eating in a restaurant with an "a la carte" menu – you can't order up the Virgin with a side of Mother and skip the Hag because you don't have an appetite for her. Later on she will come down on you.

When you are going through hard lessons from the Gods you can turn to them and say I need a break – but the longer you leave it, the harder it will be. We need to be strong – sometimes you need to strip off your clothes and look in the mirror and try to see what the Gods are trying to teach you. This is not happening outside of you - you are part of it – this is about you and for your benefit. You are the one who put your hand up and said I will do this in perfect love and perfect trust. This is a two-way thing – you choose the Goddess and she chooses you. You can't say I've come for the God, not the Goddess. You have to climb her ladder to get to him. These are very strict lessons to learn and I am still learning more about this every day of my life.

As Stuart, my mentor and my best friend, told me "You must always learn to chew the thorns before you can get to the rose."

If you look at a rose, you see a lovely green leaf. And then a long stem covered with sharp thorns. At the top of the stem is a beautiful rose, oozing with pungent beauty. That's where we want to go. But you have to start at the bottom to climb the rose. We stab ourselves with the thorns along the way and start crying. This is not what we signed up for! This is painful and bloody. I want the beautiful, smelly rose at the top, but you must suffer and learn from your mistakes first. Everything that I have achieved has been done through trial and error and it is the errors in my training that have helped me to grow.

I feel that we are all unique individuals and that the power of all our spiritual development comes from within. We are in control of our lives and our spirituality. If we need anything, all we have to do is ask the Gods. They will guide us and help us to provide our needs. However, we should to be very clear about what we think we need, as we may receive the very thing that we asked for and not know quite what to do with it. Our individual contributions to the Craft may seem small, but like little ants working together, we can move mountains and achieve great things for the world.

None greater than the Goddess and the Mighty One,

Blessed Be.

105
All the King's Children

# The Missing Ingredient

*Bronwyn*
**Third Degree High Priestess**
**United States of America**

*If we look back at each of our lives, we can often identify a turning point when everything shifts and we are sent moving unexpectedly in another direction. Sometimes this occurs as gently as if walking a path, coming to a crossroad, and realizing for the first time that the road we travel is not pre-determined but one of our own invention. Sometimes however, this is not our reality and the events that change us forever are beyond our worst nightmares and present challenges that take us to places that we never imagined we could survive. Bronwyn's story begins with just such an event – the death of her third child.*

I was raised as a Christian in Protestant churches. I went to Presbyterian churches, a Methodist church, and later to a Lutheran church. In 1972 an illness known as Rh disease caused the loss of my second child.

*Rh antigen is found on red blood cells and forms early in fetal life. However, a small percentage of people do not have this antigen on their blood cells. The antigen is a dominant genetic trait, which means that if one of the two genes that produce the antigen is positive and the other is negative, that individual will have the Rh antigen present on the red blood cells and that person will be Rh positive. If Rh positive blood is mixed with Rh negative blood, antibodies will form that will destroy blood cells that have the Rh antigen present. If an Rh negative woman and an Rh positive man produce a child, the possibility of a baby that has Rh positive blood is 60-70%. If this occurs, it could cause the mother to make antibodies against the baby's blood which effectively destroy the baby's red blood cells and the child can die.*

Following the loss of my second child to this disease, I stayed with the church. My faith in God was very strong. Losing a child was something that I could never imagine would happen to me. But I found the inner strength to deal with this death and moved on. Unfortunately, when a family loses a child, it can sometimes break people in ways that are unimaginable. People grieve differently and each member of the family manages that grief in a unique way. A few years after the death of my baby, I got a divorce from the child's father and two years later remarried. We proceeded to try and have another child.

Because I have Rh negative blood and my husband had Rh positive blood, we understood that the odds of having a healthy child were not in our favor. However, I believed that God would work things out for me. Throughout my third pregnancy, I had friends from several churches praying for me – I believed with all my heart that this child would be healthy. Unfortunately, despite how strong my faith in God was, it just didn't work out. My baby lived five days and then had a massive brain hemorrhage. We had to make the decision to take her off life support. This occurred in October of 1980.

This was the beginning of my questioning my belief in God. I had been taught that prayers are answered and that the more people praying for a positive outcome, the greater the chance that things will work out. I went back to church but all I could do was cry while I was there. I felt betrayed. Eventually I just couldn't go to church anymore so I stopped. Then my marriage broke up too. I didn't understand what was happening to me. I had been so faithful to God and He had turned His back on me. I was still spiritual but not religious. I knew I needed to believe in something but didn't know what that something was.

In 1982, I formed an organization called the Parapsychology SIG of Mensa because I had become interested in all things paranormal. Having lost a couple of children, I was particularly interested in what happens after we die. After burying two children, I wasn't sure of any of my beliefs. I was raised to believe one thing and then found out the hard way that it didn't always work out that way.

Through the parapsychology organization, I heard of a gentleman named Lewis VanDercar, who was supposed to be a witch. He was known as "The Wizard of Tampa Bay" (Florida). He was quite well known and one of my friends took me to meet him. Lewis spoke to us about truth and said that it was not a fragile thing. He encouraged us to really analyze things – to pick them apart and look at things from all angles -- because if it was Truth, it would endure. Witchcraft was presented to us as a positive belief system that was never to be used to harm anything – person or animal.

This all started to resonate with me and we would go to his home every Sunday night to hear him speak and have lively discussions. It was kind of a study group and two of my friends, Hilda and Eloise, went with me. I remember that the "Wizard" threw lavish Halloween costume parties every year with thousands of guests arriving in costume. He never referred to himself as a Wiccan, but as a Magus. It was after one of these events that I met an Alexandrian High Priestess. She would eventually become my teacher.

In talking with her, I was able to look at nature objectively for the first time. I didn't lose these children because I was being punished. I wasn't betrayed. I lost them because of the nature of my blood. I started to have peace about what had happened for the first time. I saw the God/ Goddess as living entities that I could tune into, but unlike before, these Gods were not on pedestals. I was taught how I could draw an alignment with these energies and they could work through me. Adding the concept of Goddess made a lot of sense to me because we are born male and female. It was only natural that there be a connection to female deity.

So the three of us started working with this High Priestess. She taught us the proper construction of the magic Circle, the invocation of the Watchtowers, and a lot more before Initiation. My friends were initiated a couple of weeks ahead of me. I had to go out of town that weekend so I missed it. When I came back, my own Initiation was arranged. I think it is interesting that out of the three of us, as far as I know I am the only one who went all the way to third degree. I'm not sure what Eloise is doing now and Hilda has since passed on.

I had a fire in my belly and started teaching in St. Petersburg, Florida. I had been raised to second degree at this point by the same High Priest who brought me into the Craft. I trained and initiated a full Coven of witches in St. Petersburg, including the man I would later marry.

I have one living son who is now forty-two years old. During the time I lived in St. Petersburg – in 1985 -- he had just joined the Navy. Before enlisting, he had set up an early form of Internet-like computer communication called a BBS system. My son asked his girlfriend and I to keep this BBS up and running while he was away. It was on this system that I first received a message from a person named John.

John was extremely intelligent and we built up a good rapport through our communication. I knew he was special but didn't foresee him as a future life partner. I had recently done some magic to find my soul mate. I wrote down all the qualities I wanted in a man. I had survived many bad relationships – basically I kept marrying different aspects of my father and it obviously wasn't working out, So I took the time to make a complete list of what I wanted in a man and made myself a promise to never marry again unless my husband met every single one of those requirements. The one thing that I didn't write down was age. I had married an older man before and so I knew that I could love an older man.

Because John chatted on the BBS in such a mature way, I assumed he was an adult. I asked where he worked and he told me he was still in school. So I figured he was a college student and asked him what college he went to. He answered that he had not yet graduated from high school. We met soon afterward and I really liked him. I was dealing with an "empty nest" syndrome, so I felt that he was like a surrogate son to me. John had a rough childhood and had never experienced any type of warm nurturing from a woman, so my friendship with him had a tremendous impact on him. After a while he started talking like we had a future together. I said no, this would never work – there was a difference of over twenty years in our ages. Complicating the situation even more was the fact that he had started to study the Craft with me. He had asked me to teach him and I agreed. John was really dedicated to the Craft and was a good student.

By the time John graduated from school and joined the Navy, I had – quite accidentally -- fallen deeply in love with him. When he left for boot camp, I knew that IF he came back, he would be a different person. I also knew that there was a good chance that he would not come back.

After John finished boot camp, he came back and asked me to marry him.

Much to the dismay of my family and most of his, we got privately Handfasted by our Coven and parent Coven and publicly married four days later. We've been married for over twenty-one years. John has every quality I asked for on my magical list except for that one missing ingredient. The universe was very good to me. When I share this spell with others, I always caution them that if age is important to them, be sure to write it down.

In 1993 the Navy transferred John from Florida to Nevada. It was awful for me to move from Florida where I had a Coven to a place where I didn't know anyone. The first question I asked when we got to our new home was where are the pagans? We were surrounded by Mormons and ranch families who had been living there for over a hundred years. It was really rough just to meet people. We were living over eighty miles from the city of Reno where there was a small amount of pagan activity and at least one pagan bookstore.

Eventually, through posting a flyer in our small town's bookstore, we were able to connect with a few pagans but there was definitely no British Traditional Witchcraft going on here. The eclectic pagans turned up their noses at the mere mention of a traditional regimen – they couldn't imagine that anyone would want to actually go to classes and receive training – let alone take an oath of secrecy. Eventually we moved again, this time to the mountains outside of Reno where we have lived for the past eleven years.

My husband and I are both 3rd degree Alexandrian but he is not motivated to participate much in ritual unless we have students. So in the dry spells when it was just the two of us sometimes the most I could do to worship was to go out on the deck on the full moon night and do my thing by myself. This was kind of hard for both of us. We would find people who said they wanted to learn the Craft but they didn't stay with it. A few of them even went out and told the community about our personal Craft business, which really ticked me off.

Then about three years ago it finally started to come together. We started drawing people who actually wanted to work and who were not afraid to make a commitment. We ended up with a Coven of nine students. Since growth often means change, we are now talking about part of our Coven hiving off due to a strong influence being exerted upon them by another Pantheon. I have a 2nd Degree HP who has grown enough that he is nearly ready to lead them.

I was born in Binghamton, New York. My father was a very strict man who was raised Baptist but who didn't always practice what he preached. My mother is a good Christian woman who lives her beliefs. I had a very active imagination as a child and remember that I believed in fairies. I always believed in ghosts and somehow knew even as a child that the soul endures after leaving the body at death. I was a very curious child and always had an interest in the sciences, but I also believed in God...I usually went to Sunday school on my own. I don't recall my family attending church services with me until I was about fifteen and my mother went infrequently when I was younger. I also went every summer to Vacation Bible School. I have always believed in God although I had no way of knowing at such a young age how my perception of God would be changed through future life events.

Today I view my role as a High Priestess as one of the most important roles of my life. I have always thought of myself as a teacher and will never deny someone the opportunity to learn. I consider my teaching as my Spiritual Legacy. My personal goal is to raise a family of Alexandrian Witches in the State of Nevada.

I never had the pleasure of meeting Alex Sanders so my perceptions of him are from things I've been told or have read about him. I certainly don't see him as God-like. I see him as a showman who made a lot of mistakes during his life, but nevertheless was obviously loved enough by those who practiced with him that a whole beautiful tradition of witchcraft was born from his influence. It is a wonderful thing to have this rich heritage to pass on to other people.

I believe that what is important in life is to have a relationship with something above yourself – to have a spiritual connection – and to know that when times are bad and you are hurting, you can go to your altar and pray. When a friend is sick, you can go to the altar and light candles and ask the Lord and Lady to help that person. We can do healing Circles together and people will get better.

I started off my story by telling you that I felt betrayed by God. Now I feel that I have a connection with the Gods and if I sincerely ask them to help a friend in the hospital, I see that happening. I have an amazing son and three wonderful grandchildren – all living on the other side of the country. I don't see them very often. But here in Nevada I have a spiritual family that I see every week. I know that if I have a need they will help me. I have a bond with these people that we made because of Alex. This connection is only possible because of our tradition. They need to know that they have a bond too – not just with me but with other Alexandrians.

A lot of what we do is self-improvement. Not power over people, but power within yourself -- learning to awaken what is within you. Learning to work with your own abilities and make yourself a better person. My legacy – what's truly important to me – is not what jobs I've had or where I've traveled. It's what I am teaching and what I will learn. It is what I will leave when I am gone. That's what drives me. That is more important than the jewelry I will leave to my granddaughters or the memories I will leave to my husband. When I'm gone I want people to be able to say, "You know, I'm glad I knew her. I learned some things from her. I made myself a better life because I knew this woman." That's what is important to me.

Several months ago, I was approached by a transgendered student who asked me to teach him. I hadn't any experience working with transgender students and so I asked my peers in the Alexandrian community for advice. Many Priests and Priestesses wrote to me and said follow your heart. But there were some who told me that in their opinion he was not suitable for the Craft because he had changed his gender.

I didn't understand this reaction because I have always lived my life believing that as a teacher it is not my place to deny anyone the opportunity to learn or to decide what is right for another person in terms of a spiritual path. I am happy to say that I did initiate this man and he makes me so proud. This young man, who was deemed to be unfit by men and women who never had the opportunity to know him -- simply because he was transgender -- is turning out to be one of the most fit Priests I have ever known.

I have never been afraid to follow my heart. Perhaps I am a pioneer in that regard. I go to places that others have never gone. But I believe that when we follow our heart we can never go wrong.

Teaching was easy in Florida. Students were plentiful. When we moved to Nevada, our experience here held many disappointments. There were times when I was discouraged but it never occurred to me to quit. My perseverance, like the mysterious missing ingredient in my love spell, is what pulled me through. It hasn't been easy but nothing worthwhile ever is. I feel I am finally sharing the love which I have for our beautiful tradition with students who will be moved to begin Covens of their own some day. This is my legacy and I am so happy to be able to share it with a future generation of Alexandrian witches.

# A Hundred Little Miracles

*Joseph D. Carriker, Jr.*
**Second Degree High Priest**
**United States of America**

*T*he doctor stood unobserved just outside the old woman's room. She was sitting up in bed, head down, her face turned away from him. Her right arm was pulled tightly across her chest, the fingers rolled into what appeared to be a fist which was held over her heart.

"So what is she going to do now?" he thought, "Fight me?" He was losing patience with this one. The whole purpose of admitting her to the asylum in the first place was to cure her insanity but to do that he needed to bring her to the point where she admitted she needed help. He had tried everything to bring her on board but she would not break.

He scribbled some notes onto her chart and went into the room. It was nearly dark and this was his last round of patient visits for the day. Soon he would climb into his car and start the long journey home to his family. The room was filled with twilight – not quite night but already as far from day as one could get. Southern nights came down like a curtain.

If she heard him enter, there was no acknowledgement of his presence. She kept her head down. He could hear her whispering to herself.

"Probably talking to the spirits again" he mused to himself. Many of his patients heard voices. "But this one talks to the dead too."

He stood by the side of her bed, close enough to see her lips moving silently – speaking words only she could hear.

"If you don't start participating in your own therapy, you are going to die in this asylum" he said coldly. The words were harsh but he had to do something to get her attention.

Suddenly, in a movement as quick and decisive as a deer leaping in front of a car, she opened her hand and flung it in his direction. Blood spattered over his face and chest. He jumped back in shock and disbelief.
The old woman was smiling at him.

"Well, let me tell you something boy. I may die in here but when I do, I will take you with me."

I was born in Cullman, Alabama, though raised in South Texas for the whole of my childhood.

My mother likes to say that she went directly from being "someone's daughter to being someone's wife." She married my father when she was quite young. My dad, on the other hand, was a Marine, who served two tours in Vietnam before they married. He spent most of his adult life as a shrimper, welder or off-shore oil rigman. Their marriage was rocky. He suffered from his experiences in war, and she was too young and naive to really know how to deal with his mood swings and the other things that he couldn't talk about, but could only deal with through alcohol. They split up when I was about 10 years old, and my mother pretty much raised us from that point on.

She was a hard-working woman. She'd never had to hold down a job before she was suddenly left to put food on the table by herself for two young boys. She had no education, so she got jobs bartending and waiting tables to make ends meet, all the while raising us in a small South Texas barrio. Though this neighborhood had its fair share of crime and drugs, it also had many wonderful families who stuck together and looked out for one another. In many ways, my brother and I were raised by the proverbial village, who looked out for us, and aided our mother when they could.

My mother's bravery and refusal to give up has always been an inspiration. I once told her that while my paganism might seem strange to her, it was no surprise to me that I would end up in a faith where God was a Mother - I've known no greater Divinity and Grace in my life than my mother's, and it was in my mother's eyes that I ever first saw the Goddess.

I have two younger siblings. A brother who is four years younger than I, and a sister who is thirteen years younger.

My father was not religious in the least. My mother raised us Southern Baptist, however, with a short stint in the Pentecostal church, but we were always very casual church-goers at best.

My father's family, with roots in Louisiana, always had a touch of "swamp air" to their dealings with the world, and part of that included a touch of the occult. My father's mother died in an asylum, as they claimed that the spirits she spoke with were symptoms of paranoid schizophrenia - which may or may not have been true. But she was also elbows-deep in Lousiana voodoo and root-work, and known as someone you could see if you needed "your cards thrown."

My family likes to tell the story of how she took two doctors who worked in the asylum with her when she died. One of the doctors was very dismissive of her claims that she talked with the dead. To be fair, it would have been difficult to find a doctor at that time who wouldn't have been dismissive, but this doctor apparently made her life in the asylum very difficult. One day she had enough of him, or as my grandmother used to say it, she "got her fill of him." So one day he walks into her room to find her with her hand cupped tightly over her chest. She had bitten through the membrane between her thumb and the rest of her hand and had bled into her fist. When he was close enough, she flung her hand at him which completely splattered him with her blood. From that moment on, he refused to have anything to do with her. He was replaced by a colleague who was equally difficult for her to deal with. Within two weeks of her death, both doctors died suddenly - one in a car accident and one from heart problems.

When I was young and a fervent little Christian, she told me that I was going to grow up and be a hex doctor so be careful not to listen to the pastor too much. Needless to say, I didn't take that so well at the time. But she wasn't the only magic lady in my childhood.

Growing up, the little Mexican widow who lived next door to us had a reputation in the neighborhood as a bruja. My mother claimed that she'd seen her "Devil's bible" herself before, and I have distinct memories of going over to her house, and marveling at the strange and unusual pictures on the walls, and things on the shelves. My mother even brought me to her house once when I was young and suffering from bronchitis, and I remember my chest being anointed and rubbed with olive oil, and then she rolled an egg on my chest, and cracked it to reveal a blackness in the yolk. Of course, by now, I know how this trick is done, but I also know that my lungs cleared up.

I was always the geeky kid growing up, playing Dungeons & Dragons, with my nose buried in a book. Oddly, though, these weren't the interests that led me to the occult. It was researching various religions shortly after my break with Christianity that introduced me to paganism, first in the form of Asian and Indian faiths, and then wondering if there were any faiths like those, but native to my own ethnic heritage.

My break with Christianity was a by-product of my coming out as a young gay man, at about the age of fifteen. Or rather, not coming out so much as expressing fears that I might be gay to my Southern Baptist pastor of the time. Instead of love and support, I found condemnation, and a fear that I had to be saved before it was "too late." In trying to grasp me tighter and pull me closer to their ideal of who I as a young man should be, they managed only to push me further away. I've always been a spiritual person. For a time in my youth, I strongly considered joining the clergy. For a while after that, I shoved everything to do with religion and spirituality away from me with both hands. The church had been part of my life for as long as I could remember, and in that sudden, echoing emptiness that came with my flight from Christianity, everything changed.

On some level this reaction was what I both expected and feared. I approached my spirituality in the best possible light. I wanted my experience in the church to be one of the peace and love the pastor talked about from the pulpit. My coming out was me testing the pastor. I knew what most people thought of homosexuality. So when I came to the pastor I wanted to see where his peace and love was. I hoped for the best. When I received his reaction I was more disappointed than surprised. Realizing that I was being rejected by a group of people I trusted just because of who I might fall in love with was an eye opener for me.

I've always been interested in the occult. I was an avid folklore and mythology nerd as a kid, and can remember frustrating my mother by "playing witch cottage" as a kid. I would clear out a section of the garage, and turn it into my "witch cottage" by emptying all the shelves of tools and old household detritus, and filling glass jars with plants from outside, and glass bottles with food-colored water in it. I took one of my mother's old photo albums, stripped it of photos and pasted white pages with all sorts of weird "magic" symbols and other "magic words." I carried on long conversations with imaginary animals about making sure the weather was nice, and helping the trees outside grow. Those interests carried me well into high school (though I grew out of "playing witch cottage" by the time I was 10.)

It was about that time that I found fantasy novels in the school library. I've always kept my interests in fantasy and folklore fairly separate in my mind, even though my favorite fantasy material tends to be based on real-world concepts.

For a while after I realized that the Southern Baptist thing was not going to work out, I was what I like to call a militant agnostic. My attitude was "I don't know and neither do you." I didn't feel like I had enough faith to be an atheist or to assume that our ability to discern the universe had reached its maximum and what we can sense now is the "end all, be all." I felt there was something there, but the theology was coming between me and the Divine.

In the church there was a lot of emphasis put on finding out what was "right" – there were those who were "right with God" and those who were not. The concept that I may be making the wrong choice was very real to me. If I had the resources at the time to find a Christian church that would have welcomed me as a gay man, I would have most likely ended up there. But this was South Texas and that option never presented itself. I was forced to go out in the wild so to speak to find my own way.

I did a lot of reading in high school and remember one book called the *Encyclopedia of World Religions*. The book contained a half page to a page on nearly every faith you can imagine. I was fascinated with Asia and particularly Japan, so I read a lot about Buddhism and Shinto. While reading the section on Shinto, I noticed a page reference to Western Paganism. I thought *what the heck is Western paganism?* so I jumped through the book and saw a reference to *Drawing Down The Moon* by Margot Adler. This got me to the University library to do additional hunting and I stumbled into the Craft from there.

I was living in Texas in my mid-twenties and working at a local newspaper. I had a good friend who met and fell in love with a girl over the internet, and moved to Oregon to be with her. We stayed in contact and one day he invited me to visit them. I had some vacation time to take so I headed up to Oregon. After the first week they took me Silver Falls State Park. It is a deep depression that has several rivers and streams flowing into one beautiful waterfall after another. Of course the Pacific Northwest is one big temperate rain forest and this place was gorgeous. To this day I call Silver Springs Falls Park the Notre Dame of Paganism. I said I'm moving up here and spent the last week of vacation hunting down a job.

I had been working with an eclectic group in the San Antonio area but things had fallen apart with them before I moved. Once in Oregon, I made several friends who were also pagan. One of them had recently met someone at a local shop who was the High Priest of an Alexandrian Coven and this is where I ended up.

I first read about Alex Sanders in a book. For a very long time, he was just the founder of "one of those old traditions" for me. I wasn't even aware that the Coven I eventually initiated into was Alexandrian for a while. They were simply witches that I could admire and look up to, and they had something I felt drawn to. It was only later that the name took on relevance, and then importance to me.

It's strange to say when I first entered a magic Circle, because I'd been involved in the neopagan movement for nearly a full decade before I was brought into my mother Coven. I'd certainly been in Circles before then, but looking back (with a bit of a bias, perhaps), I feel confident in saying that I wasn't in a magic Circle until perhaps my Dedication. Going through that experience was transformational, in many ways - my perspective foremost among them. Certainly, I'd been in what I would consider sacred space, but it was sacred because I chose to regard it as such. In a way, it was sacred because I mentally joined that physical space with the concept of the sacred in my mind.

My first experience in that Dedicational Circle, however, was different. I wasn't aligning the Circle with some idea in my mind. Instead, I was the one being aligned, brought into something much larger than myself, which held its sacredness in spite of what I might think.

My role as a Priest of the Craft is very different from what I once thought my role as a pastor would be. My role as a Priest is to maintain the Old Faith, to be a proper warden of the Tradition - a thing of great beauty, a subtle language for communicating things that desperately need to be said in today's world. I am a Priest of my Gods, first and only. Unlike many, I see no pastoral duties tied to this role: I am not here to be a counselor for others, nor to shepherd anyone in any capacity. Even my responsibilities to my Covenfolk and students are more like familial duties than pastoral ones, arising because kin helps kin, rather than because I'm acting on behalf of some Higher Power (or church) for someone. At the end of the day, I'm here to preserve a thing of sublime beauty, to pass it on to those who will understand and honor it in a like fashion, and to feed my Gods as I am fed by them.

Many witches come into the Craft with some form of natural talent or other gift that often forms an emphasis for them in their path here. For a very long time, I despaired because I felt that while I was a perfectly decent student, I had no such "pre-existing gifts" as a witch. Now, however, I feel that this was to my benefit. I've struggled to learn, understand and experience everything I can, and have had no natural proclivities to fall back on. As such, I feel that I understand the sorts of struggles that every student of the Craft finds themselves in the middle of at some time or another. I know that part of my own Work in the Craft is as someone who can aid in the perpetuation of what I liken to a precious family heirloom. And I consider it such: it's valuable beyond price, in some way, and so not only do I care for it well while it's in my charge, but I also have to be aware of who it is that will make a good guardian for that Craft when that time comes.

My training as a witch was at first very casual, and in a group setting. After my Dedication, it varied: sometimes personal, other times in a group setting. My High Priestess, Sophia, has always shown a remarkable ability to understand the ways that I can learn best - sometimes, even in spite of myself. I would have to say that the most intensive time of training in my history to date was when I lived at the Covenstead in southeast Portland, Oregon. We rented a large house to serve as not only a home for us, but for our Coven. In that setting, I bloomed, as every interaction - household chores, cooking a meal together, working in the garden, sitting around on the back deck - provided an opportunity for learning in some capacity. Over the years we have formalized much of our training, but have worked to avoid losing that "personal touch."

About two years ago I moved to Atlanta, Georgia to take a job with a company who makes role-playing books. I had met my partner while in Oregon and he agreed to move from the Pacific Northwest to the wilds of the South to be with me.

I am currently living across the United States from my High Priestess. I am running both an outer court group and a Coven under the auspices of my High Priestess, and continue to train under her, both long distance and in intensive sessions when we are able to visit one another. Currently, I consider my most active training to be the lessons learned running and organizing both Coven and court, and I stay in constant contact with her about everything.

I used to have grand visions about my future as an elder of the Craft, but truthfully, I hope to accomplish what other witches have accomplished - a happy life surrounded by people I love, pinpointed with the occasional opportunity to use our Craft to make a positive difference. I want to pass this beautiful gift on to others who will cherish it the way I do, and to live a life of love and joy, because that is our true service to the Gods of the Wicca.

Alex Sanders was our King. Of course, when I say that, I do so in full recognition of what a scoundrel he often was, while simultaneously being an amazing witch and magus. I fully believe that Alex was a King - but a King of Misrule. His attention-seeking, his love of grand stories, spectacle and meeting new people (and sometimes initiating them quickly thereafter) taught the elders of our Craft, whether he intended to or not. Most of all, though, his love for the Goddess was deep and abiding, and is the witch-blood that courses through our spiritual bodies as surely as the red blood of our families is what courses through our physical ones.

People sometimes ask me to point out that one experience in my life which rises above all the others. There isn't any single one.

There have been a hundred little ones, though: the joy of seeing people I love and adore take steps into their own power and deepening their connection with the Tradition in Initiation and elevation Circles; finding my own feet beneath me after an early life that did nothing to prepare me to accept both responsibility and power for myself; the hundred little miracles that are part and parcel with touching the Old Power in the witch's way. Perhaps one of the most significant experiences I ever had was attending one of the Alexandrian Teas, in years past, and feeling the deep, abiding connection linking every person there. Complete strangers, in many cases, coming together in shared experience, exploring roots that connect deep out of sight, but that anchor us just as surely as anything else could.

The witch's Will is what matters most. Call it effort, or belief. Call it what you will. Witches are willing to fly in the face of adversity, of difficulty and even failure. They refuse to just shrug and sink back below the waters, pulled down by an undertow of powerlessness. We have seen and touched the Old Power, and while we may tire of the constant dog-paddling we have to do in order to stay afloat, we do it because we know it's real and genuine.

One of the things I tell my students is that to do this, to pursue Initiation and the work of the Priesthood, you have to be one of two things – you have to be completely insane or have no other choice. The initiatory process is such a crucible. We deliberately choose to begin a series of spiritual and occult mechanisms that will break us down completely so we can rebuild ourselves. But this process is also fraught with heartache. There are so many tears that move the process forward. In a very real way even if I had it to do all over again, I would. I am grateful to have had this experience.

Val (on the right in the turned down wellies) with
her sister Gail

The Daughter of Pan

*Val Hughes*
**Third Degree High Priestess**
**Wales**

Wben I first realized that I wanted to be connected to the divine, I also quickly realized that conventional routes were closed to me as they did not resonate with me at all. The priests of the Christian religion were said to have direct contact but it was my experience that, far from being facilitators, they seemed to be barriers to God and truth. This moment of enlightenment was critical to my spiritual development because it was through this inner knowing that I experienced the Knowledge of God. However, it had no tangible expression or frame of reference in which to teach me about its self.

I had this sort of idea, this sort of feeling about god and godliness. As much as I wanted to talk about these feelings, I understood that people generally did not discuss these things. What little I was able to learn from the priests about God was very dry and didn't speak about inner life. I learned the scriptures but they were only a code of conduct and didn't talk about development, about a connection with the divine. God was a separate entity – something certainly very foreign. I tried various means to get some sort of connection but it just did not happen.

This longing to connect increased after the birth of my child. I think there is this secret club that women belong to once they have a child. It's a bit like initiation – you can never really tell someone how fabulous they will feel until they experience it. I had a huge high after my son was born – and I knew there was no way this was not connected to the source of life. I didn't know it by this name but it was divine – a spark of life. That has to come from somewhere – it can't be just biology.

I was born in Wales in 1958. My parents were Welsh. My father (a Capricorn) was intelligent, quite an eccentric, a very brave soldier, a hunter and a hard working man. My mother (a Pisces) was a funny, intuitive little woman. She was quite a worrier who instilled in her children a sometimes over concern with consciousness of others. When I was six years old and my sister eight, the family moved and our lives changed forever. My mother took over a business with the help of one of our two eldest sisters, the other left for college and my brother to join the army, so my sister Gail and I were very much left to our own means. Some say we were left to run wild!

My sister and I together were greater than the sum of our parts. We reached very odd conclusions about things, we discussed our dreams as reality. There were just two of us and we grew up in a very small community. We were country bumpkins, not worldly at all although we aspired to be somehow.

When we were young children my father worked as a forester. During the school holidays my mother would often pack us off to work with him. We would pile into the land drover with our lunch and the dog and head off to the depths of the forest – what adventures! Dragons, witches, hounds of hell, giants, our imagination knew no bounds. At the end of the day my father's work horse, Lizzi, (they were always named Lizzi, for the Queen) who was about 18 hands would be liberated of her collar and chains and sent back to her stable which was usually a couple of miles away. She was normally sent on her own as with that special horse sense, she always found her way. Our special treat at the end of the day was to ride her home. My father would lift us onto her broad back, me at the front, my sister behind. He'd slap Lizzi's backside and off we'd go. When I think of it now it was outrageous! Two little girls of 5 and 7 on a giant brown beastie, bareback with no bridle, but I had not a care in the world. I was safe within my sisters loving arms and nothing could harm me.

My sister and I were very much left to our own means as children and immersed ourselves in a magical world of monsters under the bed and special trees where we would make wishes and leave gifts of sixpences for the fairies, which were always accepted. (Unbeknown to me, my sister would later return and pocket the money!) I was always the gullible person. I thank my lucky stars for how well things turned out for me. Coming into the Craft and magic the way that I did, anything could have happened. I was very lucky. My sister didn't develop the same interests in the occult as I did. She remains an incredibly intuitive person and is very wise. She has this intuitive way of knowing.

When I was a child my mother and her sister were Ouija board practitioners and my sister and I used to listen and watch. (We used to keep very quiet, so we were not noticed.) Later as teenagers we practiced it for ourselves. This was stopped as we started to get results and my sister became concerned.

My parents were a bit less religious than average for Welsh people of their time. I was christened in the Chapel as were my siblings. In those days Wales was "dry" on Sunday's. (no alcohol to be sold anywhere) and my father had to drive into England to visit a pub. A vote was taken in Wales to see if this law could be amended but, to my father's disgust, the chapel voted against Sunday pub opening and so he moved us all to church in protest!

We were much happier, as the vicar and his wife were very community minded and lots of events, outings and youth clubs were now open to us. This happy state of affairs, alas, was short lived and the vicar was moved to a larger parish and was replaced by an altogether different man. He took an instant dislike to me on our first meeting when I asked him why Mary was called the "Virgin" Mary. Further annoyances followed with such questions as: Why were we born in sin - what did that mean?

In retrospect I think I was probably quite a precocious child, one that adults found uncomfortable to be around and too "knowing." I seemed to know when adults were hiding things or being dishonest. As my sister and I were left to our own devices we were a bit backward at hiding our thoughts and feelings and would blurt out inappropriate comments, usually to the shame of our mother, but invariably true.

Returning to my experience of church and Sunday school: on one occasion we were being shown pictures of bible stories, Daniel in the lion's den etc., when the teacher displayed a picture of the devil, red, with forked tail and horns, a hush fell around the vestry and she announced "Yes…. We all know who this is don't we- Valerie Hughes?" Insinuating, of course, that from my general behavior that I would already, at the age of six, have intimate knowledge of the diabolic! So from an early age horned beings have had great influence on my life! I can still remember the teacher's voice – it was so disapproving. What a dreadful terrible thing to do to a small child.

I think I knew I was an outcast from that moment on.

I was told about witchcraft in 1979 but didn't understand. My only knowledge was of the persecutions. Witches didn't really exist.

It took me a while to realize that this meant there was a direct link through the feminine to the divine.

I truly believe that the greatest magic we can do is within ourselves. My primary focus has remained one of self-discovery through the wonderful mysteries of the Craft. Recently I cared for someone who was dying. My training as a priestess certainly helped in this. I felt the Goddess move through me to show compassion and love and to make sure that this person didn't die alone. Currently my role is very much that of teacher.

I must admit that perpetuation of the Craft has not been the driving force behind any of my actions. If I have an active role in this, it is in trying to provide my initiates with a sound magical basis to explore the mysteries for themselves. I do think over popularization of Craft does make it more accessible, but also dilutes the quality of initiates.

Other factors and events in my life as an adult and an initiate have taught me that without a self knowledge or self reliance we are doomed to fail. The urge to penetrate the mysteries is a solitary path. Of course we have partners and other initiates who accompany us on the way but ultimately our spiritual quest leads us to the self. It is our inner self we are seeking the union is within. I think I have always known this but discovering magic confirmed it for me. When a person strives too much for a group experience it is easy to miss seeing the person in the mirror.

In any creation myth - however you look at it – there is an "itness" - god or whatever we want to call it. Then this god force splits from itself in order to have knowledge of its self. We are part of this split and then must find our way back. If we are not estranged from it, we can never have a consciousness of the divine. As a child a real roadblock for me was the story of the Garden of Eden. I never understood why God would punish people who seek Knowledge.

One of my most memorable encounters with deity came in 1984 when I attended an outdoor midsummer ritual. This was the first time I witnessed the Horned God of the witches invoked into the circle. To see the God manifest was a powerful and life changing experience for me. I wasn't prepared for this experience as I didn't know that much about the Craft. It is still difficult to find words to describe the effect it had on me. I spent the next three years trying to assimilate what I had witnessed "in a place wild and lone" with what I had read of Craft. Dreams and nightmares of horned hunters of the night haunted me for months. I had dreams of invoking Pan and then feeling that rush of energy that I had come to associate with the God. I was attracted and frightened at the same time. This combination of excitement and terror, of feeling elated and then wanting to go and hide, was all very confusing. My subconscious was really trying to deal with this.

At the time I was living alone in the country in the middle of nowhere. One night I had a very intense dream in which I invoked Pan. Then I heard him approaching. I struggled within the dream with primal fear – of knowing that who I had invoked had answered my prayers and was coming to me in response to my invocation. Then I realized that I was no longer dreaming and that I lay awake in my bed. It was just before dawn and the light was starting to shimmer on the horizon. I thought to myself "oh no, I'm awake." And I could hear Pan in the distance – getting closer and closer. My heart was pounding and I looked to the window which faced out on the slope of a hill. I dared myself to get out of bed, to go to the window, and look out. Every movement took all of my will and courage.

When I finally moved the curtain and looked outside, I saw a very old ram caught in a thicket of wood halfway down the hill. He bleated pitifully for me to help him. Unfortunately he died a few days later.

Now I understand the meaning of Pan. One of his names is Pandemonium and he is not the happy horned God of the witches. He represents life but also death. And to know him is to know both – you can't pick one and not the other. These are not easy lessons.

I was initiated in 1987. When I asked for initiation, my teacher and I (who was an initiate of Alex and Maxine and also a neophyte of the Egyptian mysteries) were visiting the British Museum in London. I asked for initiation just as we went through the pillars at the entrance, he said yes and immediately turned into the Egyptian room and put me to stand before a statue of Sekhmet and explained that if my heart wasn't true, she would endeavor to rip it out! Training was tough in those days!

It had taken me so long to build up the courage to ask him for initiation.

He asked me "Why have you taken so long?" I said I was scared and he nodded and said "Yes". I knew I should be scared and that the training was not going to be easy.

Today I lead a training Coven in Shropshire, England.. As well as providing the best training to my students as I possibly can, there is very much more I would like to discover by myself, for myself. I am currently exploring Astral Temple work and returning to my first love – Hermetics. When I think of Alex, I realize he left one hell of a legacy. I have felt the presence of Alex in circles and now understand the Gardnerian use of the toast to the "old ones." A most curious series of events unfolded during the search for a name for our current Temple, we now believe these to have been guided, if not by Alex, then by his namesake.

The idea of being challenged frightens some people. Our biggest learning curve is when we are challenged. Some people start off wanting to learn the Craft but they leave soon after. I used to think "why did they leave?" but then I realized that some people don't need to go any farther in one lifetime We can't look at everyone in the same context – this isn't a four year university course. If you fail or stop it doesn't mean something is wrong with you. Alex initiated hundreds of people and some never came again – that was his job. He lifted us all up by opening the floodgates – the great occultists before him lifted our consciousness up and then Alex came along and took us up again.

Some readers may find this book and see in it a message of hope. If they read this book and are inspired by it, that might be enough. By reading about the experiences of others they will expand their own awareness. Sometimes it is not possible for people to have an awareness of what their path will be because it changes as we develop. The path can change as we are walking it by its very definition. But walking it will always lead you forward.

I think a lot of teachers try to whitewash the Craft by putting a fresh coat of paint on it to make it more palatable. They present very complex theories in an academic way. They take all of it and break it down into a body of learning that misleads people into thinking that, if they start here, they will end up there. Everyone ticks off their boxes – done that, now I will do this.

I don't teach this way. The learning experience has to be teased out by practice – by doing. A good student will see things in different ways than the teacher because their contacts speak to them in different ways. We all know when we've been touched by the gods. A teacher can share knowledge and help students to understand, but they must never underestimate the student's own ability to experience the gods in a personal way. The end of all their searching is to make that divine connection for themselves and we can't take that away.

I believe strongly in the well known words from the Charge of the Goddess "Keep pure your highest ideals, strive ever towards them." If we are to remain true to Craft, if we really are true initiates, we will be tested, our wits will leave us, we will have our hearts ripped out and we will worship at the empty shrine. But would I do it all again? You betcha!

# Come What May

*Phoenix*
**Third Degree High Priest**
**United States of America**

*P*hoenix *is the last person I interview for this book. Even though we live in the same town, barely a mile apart, our schedules are both so crazy that it takes an effort to be sitting quietly together in the same room.*

*"Where were you born?" I start.*

*"In a manger," he responds flatly. I look up at him and he gives me one of the amazing smiles he is so famous for – it is a smile that is so unexpected that when it arrives it is like a burst of sunlight in a thunderstorm.*

*"Not buying that?" he laughs, "how about Newark, New Jersey It was 1966."*

My parents were divorced before I knew what that meant and that fathers were even part of the process. My father had other kids after the divorce so I have half brothers and sisters somewhere. Before the divorce, my mother and father had three kids – one girl and two boys. My mother is now living with my brother.

My mom is sort of born again, but not fanatic. She knows about my life and religion and is OK with it. She never forced religion on any of us. We were free to choose what we will. I am the oldest child. My brother and sister are one and two years younger, respectively. I think I'm the oldest of my half-siblings too.

My grandmother was very religious and dragged us to church every Sunday. When I was older, I started the rebellion and my mom took my side. She agreed if church didn't work for me why should I be forced to sit there. As a child I was drawn towards energy working.
Energy in and of itself is a big part of my personal work and practice. As a child I did shields and energy sensing on instinct. I kept projecting energy and drawing it in like breathing. It wasn't long before I linked these abilities to magic. Energy was my source and magic became my tool to control and direct it.

When I went to church, I didn't feel the same energy currents that I expected to experience, like I saw in movies like *The Ten Commandments.* Church was not like the images of angels I saw in the Bible or as interesting as the myths of the Gods of Egypt, Greece and Rome. In church I saw finger pointing and people who wanted me to think their way as much as they wanted me to give up my allowance every Sunday.

I had a precognitive flash as a child. I was about eleven years old.

We were all supposed to be sleeping. I was with my sister, brother and three cousins. We were singing the classic "Row, Row, Row your Boat" when it hit me. When it was my turn to sing, I was gone. I saw my mother running from her bedroom, through the house. She was on fire. She crashed through the front room windows onto the front porch and I saw her burn into a skeleton. The vision ended up with a burning skull. To this day that vision has never left my mind's eye. I was snapped out of it by my siblings and cousins shaking me and asking what was wrong and why was I crying. All I could keep saying is "she's burning up, she's burning up!"

Two weeks later my mother fell asleep with a cigarette in her hand. If it wasn't for my uncle sneaking into the house late at night and seeing the flames in her room, the vision would have come to pass. I keep seeing the vision from her perspective too. She told us what happened and how she scared she was to wake up to a pillar of fire right between her legs. I shudder to think what would have happened if my uncle had been delayed just a few more minutes. Thank the Gods something moved my uncle to the right place at the right time.

The fire vision stuck with me and after that event I could sense my own energy field and aura. The Greek and Egyptian pantheons fascinated me and when I first read and heard the words "telepathy, telekinesis, ESP, psychic and precognition" I went to the library to look up books on these subjects to learn as much about them as I could. It was like following breadcrumbs until I found gold.

As a child I was able to perceive my own energy as well as the energy of people around me. I feel auras more than I see them. Sometimes this happens in colors, but more often than not I feel the energy in the same way that one can perceive static electricity. The field's strength and "pattern" is how I can read differences and read people.

My first time in a magic Circle was as a child when I did a spell. We had moved to a new home in Newark, New Jersey. There was a series of break-ins in my neighborhood and right up the street an elderly man was murdered. I feared for my family and instinctively did a home protection and blessing. We lived in a tight neighborhood and people were always on their porch, but I didn't care.

I did a Circle and put my psychic pentagram ward on and went around the entire house using dust from the basement, dirt from the backyard, and leaves from the trees over the front sidewalk. I had created a powdered mix of these elements and, with my young mind and will, worked the mix and placed it at each of the five points outside of the house. I ended the spell with a final "lock" at the center of the home in the basement. I went totally on instinct and let myself be guided. I didn't even research the spell first. I believe we are able to use collective subconscious when we need to. The spell worked and the police caught the bastards who were doing the break-ins.

As I remember it, my first awareness of Alex Sanders and Alexandrian witchcraft came as a result of the research I had been doing about the Craft. There were many photographs of Alex in the books I read. I kept returning to his images again and again. Just as I was able to perceive energy around living things, these photographs projected energy as well. There was something about Alex that fascinated me and sparked a remembering spirit in me. He felt familiar to me, like I had known him in some other lifetime. I always knew I wanted to be an Alexandrian witch. It's like realizing you like chocolate cake over vanilla, even though you've tasted neither.

My partner is also interested in traditional witchcraft and introduced me to an Alexandrian Priest. I was disappointed with the narrow mentality of this individual. He questioned my interest in the Craft and suggested that because of my ethnicity I should study voodoo instead. My knee jerk reaction was that, if this is what he was teaching, I wanted no part of it. We should all be able to see beyond the surface and recognize that children of the Goddess come in many variations. So I never stopped just because of one person's unilluminated perceptions.

But the Gods did not fail me. Another Alexandrian High Priest, who had been living out of State for a while, returned to Massachusetts and started a training Coven. It is there that I found my home.

I became officially initiated into the Craft in Boston around 1998. I remember a few nights before I was to be initiated, I had a strange dream. I was running down a street with a high school classmate. The street was long and filled with fog and mist. The fog was thick and we turned down a narrow path like an alley way but I could not make out any actual buildings around us. I was soon aware that we were running from a pair of giant black dogs. We came to what seemed like a dead end - the fog and darkness closed in around us. I could hear the dogs behind us – getting closer. There was nowhere to run.

Instinctively I turned and pushed this classmate behind me. The two giant dogs closed in and started circling us. I thought it was strange that I was protecting this person. We were never actually close in real life, but I felt I had to keep him safe. The dogs growled and barked and then after a while became silent. Suddenly I saw an elderly woman with short white hair walk toward us. She was wearing a white blouse, buttoned to the neck and a long skirt. I couldn't see her feet because the two dogs had moved in front of her. I could see clearly that the dogs belonged to her. I stared at her and she stared back. Her face held no expression. I knew she was something, or someone, else. I didn't understand the significance of the dream until much later. I now believe the woman was a certain aspect of the Goddess who had come to test me and claim me as her own. I was accepted by her. I was loved by her. I knew I could finally become a Witch.

On the day of my Initiation, I awoke with excitement and wonder. I was also a little apprehensive about what type of ordeal I would be required to face. It was February and it had snowed a lot the night before. I hate snow with all my being and we had just had a blizzard. I got up, showered and dressed in my warmest clothes. I took nothing but water, as I had been fasting. Anxiously, I gathered up my gear and started over to my High Priest's home. I did not know what to expect. He met me in front of his home and instead of going inside he told me we were going to take a walk...in the snow. I thought...OK...

We walked for about an hour or so all over Boston, we talked and I was shown sights and things I never really quite took the time to see or notice before. Despite the snow I was enjoying the walk and started to understand that I was on a journey. Before I knew it, we wound up at North Station in Boston. Curve ball number two!

My High Priest bought two train tickets...one way...and told me to sit down. It was at this point I realized what this all meant to me and how much I both admired and trusted him. I was being initiated on many levels and was not turning back now. Come what may, I was in his hands and in the Grace of the Goddess.

I was shown a book I was not allowed to read before and I was like a kid in a magic shop. Soon our train arrived and the book was taken away from me. I was told to remain silent and meditate from this point on. I obeyed. The ride was short, about twenty minutes, and when we reached the stop I saw that we were in Salem, Massachusetts. I was a little confused. We didn't know anyone in Salem and I couldn't figure out why we were there. I think it started to snow again as we got off the train. I was led to a parked car which I did not recognize. A hooded figure was in the driver's seat. Blessed moon cakes, I was in trouble now!

I was placed in the back seat and blindfolded. I can't remember if it happened before I got in, or if I was told to put it on while in the car.

I remember thinking "Oh geez, please don't get pulled over." But it was a snowy day and not many cars were on the road. I calmed down and heard myself saying "Perfect Love and Perfect Trust." We drove for about 15 minutes and then came to a stop.

The blindfold remained on and I was led through the door of a house and up a narrow set of stairs to a second floor. We walked through a room and into a small bathroom where I was stripped and dipped. I still had no clue where I was or what to expect. Finally I was left skyclad, wrapped only in a blanket in the center of a small room. I was still blindfolded and heard movements and commotion all around me. I was given a warm brew to drink that had a little kick to it. Then suddenly the noises stopped. Suddenly a word came to me, whispered in my mind quietly but firmly. I knew this was my new name. Then the commotion began again and I had my cup snatched from my hands. I was helped to stand up. The blanket was thrown off and I was bound. The time had arrived for me to come home.

Today I run a Coven with my partner in Salem, Massachusetts. We are living in the so-called Mecca of Witches. To live here, you are involved one way or the other with community politics, whether you want to be or not. Salem can be a whirlwind of out of control egos and witch wars. But Salem is also a place filled with magic and history. When people come to Salem they sometimes expect so much more because of what Salem represents. When I say that Salem is the Mecca of Witches I mean it in a very tongue-in-cheek way. But the reality is that Salem should be a place where magical people can live, find community, and can learn from each other.

There are a lot of people in Salem looking for traditional training. This is exciting but also sad, because many of these people become disillusioned when they discover that, from the perspective of many Salem witches, if you want to be a witch you have to pay. The Alexandrian tradition doesn't charge for teaching. But one thing I learned early on is that if someone is coming to Salem they have to bring a checkbook. And that is a sad reputation for this particular town to have.

People talk about the Craft being in danger of extinction. Well, to be honest, I'm not going to stand on a soap box and shout that the Craft is in peril and blah blah blah, because it's not. It has survived all this time, for centuries. Do we honestly think it will dwindle now? But I do believe that to perpetuate the growth and evolution of the Craft requires us all to evolve.

Students are more exposed today to both crap and good material.

They ask questions and expect answers. So we, as teachers, have to take a step down off our pedestals and get into the grind with them. We need to show them truth. The work needs to be done by all of us on all levels and we each need to do our part. I also realize that teaching is not for everyone. It is hard work. It can be insane at times dealing with group dynamics. A teacher needs a lot of patience. We are all visionaries and should follow our paths in our own way.

I have a student who runs a pagan forum and actually teaches pagan kids in the "Bible Belt" no less. She asked me one day something I could not answer. She was speaking about the Alexandrian tradition on a forum and one person asked her "What have Alexandrians accomplished as a tradition in the world?" She asked me the same question and I could not give her an answer.

I couldn't think of any major landmarks she could have shared and I felt backed into a corner. After thinking about her question, I don't think we should have to prove our worth to anyone. Accomplishments can't always be measured in an obvious way. Perhaps a better question is not what do we show the world, but what will we show future generations of those who come to the Craft?

There are two characteristics that drive me – the need to find my truth and an insatiable hunger for knowledge. Every experience I have had in my life has brought results on some level and pushed me further. I was a solitary Witch and Magician for many years. This was my truth and a world that I created. Finding a group, let alone a tradition, was never at the top of the list for me. But experience brought me the Alexandrian tradition and I learned the value of Initiation and the special companionship that only a Coven family can bring.

Now that I lead my own Coven, I try to bring this same sense of family to my students. Well, my nickname among the "kids" is Papa Phoenix. I am now raising future Priests and Priestesses of the Craft who will in turn cultivate future generations to come. This is now our truth and a world that we create together. I tell my students – the Craft is not a hobby. It is your life.

I want to pass on my experiences to my students. The teachings of Alex and Maxine Sanders continue to inspire me, but I like to add a little of my own spices to the recipes. It is important to be innovative and improve further upon the teaching we received. The challenge of a teacher is not to find a student but to find a student that will take the tradition to the next level.

When I think of the "King of the Witches" I know this title belongs to someone I never knew, but admire very much. Alex Sanders was, and is, my vision and voice. To see him on video or hear his voice in a recording moves me to my core. I feel a connection to him that I can only attempt to explain. I feel like I was his student in another life. My perception of him is that he was a man of honor but also of realism. He seems personally to me like someone who has reached "sainthood" and I should acknowledge that.

Meeting Maxine Sanders was hands down the most significant experience of my life. This was a major milestone for me, and a humbling honor. Imagine how profound it is to meet one of the originators of your path – someone who you only knew from books. All my life I read books about Gods and Goddesses. Meeting Maxine was like meeting the Goddess sitting in my living room. It doesn't get any better than that. I was so star struck, I didn't know what to say.

I always tell my Coven members to persevere. When in doubt, fear and uncertainty can creep in. In adversity you have to stay true to yourself or it will get worse. For me, magic is the great equalizer. It calms me down. I'm always fond of saying that without my magic, I would be on a roof with an Uzi.

I hear of people leaving the Craft and it makes me angry. They have some issue, or go through a dark night of the soul and they fold. Some even become born again Christians. They give up. They quit. I know I shouldn't be all that annoyed since it's their life when all is said and done, but to me it shows not only a shattered faith but a lack of confidence. They let the mundane win.

I have had lots of difficult times in my life and still do. But the Craft is as natural to me as breathing, and to say I'm not going to do this anymore is something I can't fathom. I can't understand why, when people are faced with a serious issue, they turn their back on the Craft and rush back to the Christian God. I am a hardcore witch and don't see the logic in this. What are they saying? That the Craft brought them these problems? I am not living the high life myself, but I will always remember who I am and what I am and I will never give up.

I believe that witches are born – not made. When you are a Witch you don't have to wait until Halloween to say "I'm a witch." There are a lot of people in the Craft who fake it. Maybe they are here because they think it is a cool thing. Maybe I sound elitist, but you can't become a witch by picking up a book or writing a check for $300 to just anybody without looking at their past qualifications and credentials.. Actions speak louder than words. It is easy to recognize those who follow the path of the Goddess. We know our own.

All Rabbits Go to heaven

*Tanith*
**Third Degree High Priestess**
**United States of America**

*I* realized around the age of eight that there were problems with my birth religion, Catholicism. I dearly loved my rabbit and when he died, I didn't accept that he couldn't go to heaven because animals have no souls. I was so distressed by this that the Priest at my Catholic Christian Doctrine class told me that, well, perhaps in this case God might make an exception. This was definitely the moment when I realized that not only were there some very important variances between Catholicism and my perceived reality, there were also some negotiable areas even within its taught theology. Pragmatist that I am, I decided to go with my gut from that point on.

This turned out to be more than a turning away of what I had been taught – it became a multidirectional turning point. I suppose each of us become aware in our childhood that we are different from other people. In my case, I found that most of the other children went along with what they were taught. I was aware at a young age that it was OK to ask questions. Even as a little girl of only eight years of age, there was a sense of internal Gnosis that drove me to stand up for what I sensed rather than swallow what I was told.

I suppose everyone buys a party line at some point in their lives, but for me there was always a sense of inner knowing that kept bringing me back to a way of thinking that was certainly different from others, but one that I knew was true. I doubt if there are a lot of kids even today who would challenge a Priest, but I was concerned about my rabbit. I put my hand up and said "You just said animals don't go to heaven. So where did my rabbit go?" The Priest just wasn't ready for that.

I was born in Boston, Massachusetts to a Catholic father and a Unitarian mother. Both were liberal religiously. My father took us to church every Sunday and had us go through the childhood sacramental process. He was sort of a natural pagan himself, so he didn't mind when I decided around age fourteen to not go to church anymore. He never knew about my Craft affiliation.

I loved Disney movies from the time I was a toddler, with Pegasus and fairies, beautiful sparkles and talking animals. When I learned to read, I read everything, but my favorite books were fairy tales, myths, magical and ghost stories.

I'd read Sybil Leek's *Diary of a Witch* when I was about twelve, after having read of her psychic work in Hans Holzer's collections of ghost-hunting tales. I loved Sybil's life story and realized at that point what

I was myself, but didn't read Holzer's *Truth About Witchcraft* until a couple of years later.

When I was about fifteen years old, I heard a radio show on a Boston station, WBCN. The show was called *Witchcraft Weekend* and featured special guest Louise Huebner. Between songs Louise would make pithy comments about witchcraft in what seemed like an echo chamber recording. I called the radio station and told whoever answered the phone that I wanted to be a witch. He asked how old I was and when I told him he suggested I wait a couple more years. I was frustrated and disappointed, but had to take his advice. When I was seventeen I saw an ad in a local newspaper called *The Phoenix* and responded to the people who had placed the ad. I had an interview, was given a reading list, and then some back and forth until the decision was made to initiate me.

In today's world people do the public ritual thing. They have an opportunity to experience ritual without making any sort of personal commitment. We didn't have that. My first experience with witchcraft was my first-degree Initiation. Back in 1971, that was how you did it.

It was a very powerful experience, as you hadn't any previous knowledge of how things felt in a Circle in real time. I thought I had some idea of what was going to happen because I had read a few books such *The Sixth Sense* by Justine Glass. But in these books the writers sort of skated around the subject of Initiation. A lot of what I read was about magical theory such as Gerald Gardner and Margaret Murray - no one ever wrote "this is what is actually going to happen to you." I do recall being told I would have to be skyclad for a large portion of the ritual and that I would be blindfolded. So I went in knowing that.

Honestly, if these people had been nuts I would have been dead and my parents would have had no idea what had happened. I was a very bad girl that night – I told them I was going to see the Rolling Stones movie *Gimme Shelter* with some friends in Boston. Then I left home, and followed my handwritten directions to the High Priestess' apartment. I can still remember walking from the subway to her home. I was so excited – I thought, *I am finally in!*

I was not present when they cast the Circle – I was in the other room. I went in blindfolded in perfect love and perfect trust. There were clouds of incense smoke – frankincense and myrrh – I think it ironic that, Catholic as I was, I had never smelled this incense before. I remember bells were struck and anointing done. I answered as I had been coached.

At the end I was rich – more than I can ever explain. We shared food after and talked and I still got home before curfew. I still had the anointing oil on when I got home and remember thinking this was something really big.

Today I try to live the principles. I don't lead a Coven, or belong officially to one, but attend as a guest as often as I can. I see my role as a Priestess these days as using what I've learned over the years to help the people around me, or those the Gods have put in my way, to live more fully and happily. I see and feel things a lot of regular people don't. I see myself as a solitary urban wise-woman, a resource.

For mundane people I am not out. I have a policy with myself that I will never lie to a direct question, but no one ever asks me. People talk to me all the time – people with problems unload to me and I try to offer them whatever help I can. It doesn't necessarily have to be magical help. I think they respond to the Priestess in me – even though they would not know to use that reference. Actually if I did tell them, "You can talk to me, I'm a High Priestess of the Goddess", automatic flags would go up which would prevent them from being so open.

I believe that each generation re-invents the Craft. Having spent forty years on the inside, I've observed a lot of change. Every ten years or so old arguments and discussions re-surface. With fresh insight, things change and there becomes a new norm. Everything evolves – every generation brings fresh energies and new ideas. What matters is that we stay strong at the core – that the magic is always there.

There will always be plenty of voices trying to shout that down. Right or wrong, things do change - maybe there's no way around this. But what was always there remains to be re-discovered by each generation - like a platonic ideal. And in finding it all again, we make it our own.

I believe that power finds its way. This is really a testament to the strength and enduring nature of the Craft, that the core doesn't change. It is from this center that we all draw comfort. We go back to this source for energy –it is a magnificent thing.

Alex Sanders is the founder of this feast. We all go back to this same traditional image of the thing we all share, regardless of how our practices vary or how different we are. Ultimately we all draw from this single memory – like harking to a tuning fork.

I met Alex two or three times. He was funny and charming and flamboyant and generous. I picked up a box recently that I use to keep seeds in – it is a jewelry box that Alex gave me. It is funny that I picked this up in middle of this project.

I was usually very quiet when I visited Alex. One day he said "Wait a minute" and went trotting off. He came back with a jewelry box – it looked kind of French and had a lid that lifted off. The cover had little panels of scenes with Greek Gods. He said quietly "Take this and don't tell Maxine." I thanked him and brought it home. For a while I had magical jewelry in it and then I thought seeds were more appropriate.

Alex was in this place but not of this place. He seemed to have a different relationship with "stuff" than most people. It interests me that he decided of all the things he had, I of all people should get this particular object. I would like to find a way to tell Maxine about the jewelry box, though. She may have been looking for it all these years.

The last time I saw Alex, he was pretty ill. I kept thinking at the time that living so large, channeling so many energies for so many people and being out there took a toll on him. If he had lived a more self-preserving kind of life, he might have lived a longer life – he died too young. Alex gave so much that he took it out of himself physically. He was generous and cheery when I saw him – still cracking jokes. He was a man who made the most out of life and lived the best from wherever he was standing.

There is a lot of talk nowadays about the survival of the Craft. I suppose I've always seen the Craft as largely taking care of itself. Because of this, I see no need to proselytize. I believe the maxim that "witches are born, not made". I think it's important to document in writing the processes of individuals (as you are doing here), save magical texts and objects, and be available for questioning and teaching when asked. But as I said before, each generation reinvents a large part of the Craft, for better or worse. Something gets lost, something else steps in. When young people feel the call to the Craft, they'll find the teachers and material.

My focus is to keep on as I've been, to help others as the Gods see fit, and work towards having a home that guests perceive as a working and living temple. I want to live my life as an example so those with need can see all the deeper possibilities of life.

I'm one of those people who give myself more problems than I need to – just dealing with the necessities of life takes its toll. I live alone and choose not to seek another partner at this time unless my absolute soul mate comes along. Of course living alone makes it harder. It's harder to get everything done; I spread myself thin and am sometimes over extended and very tired.

One of my favorite movies is a children's film called *The Neverending Story*. At the end of this film, one of the main characters, the

Child Empress, has just a small piece of her magical kingdom in her hand. Her land has crumbled away because people stopped believing in magic. All she has left is a single grain of sand. If she loses this, everything is lost. So she holds onto that little piece of life as tightly as she can and hopes for the best. Sometimes it feels like my own kingdom is crumbling, but I do everything I can to keep holding on to what remains, and believing. I also hope for the best.

# The Constant Heart

*Oskar Majda*
**First Degree Priest**
**Poland**

*If you ask a college graduate to identify Kazakhstan on a world map, there may be some hesitation despite the fact that it is the ninth largest country in the world. Its overall geography is greater than all of Western Europe combined with terrain that ranges from desert to rocky canyons to snowy mountains. The Republic of Kazakhstan is a mysterious country with its roots springing from the blood of the nomadic tribes who once traveled across the ever changing face of the land in search of home.*

*It is during a journey of a somewhat different kind that Oskar begins his story.*

My parents worked in Kazakhstan as diplomats for four years and I visited them many times while there. On each of these visits they would try to provide me with exposure to the culture of the country, which often included organized trips across the country to see historic sites. Kazakhstan is a country with a rich and interesting past. There are a lot of relics there from ancient cultures, including ruins and cave drawings which are not widely known to European and American people.

On this particular day we were on a journey to see the famous 14th century Buddhist rock drawings on the canyon walls high above the Ili River. We were traveling with a few people from the Embassy. It was a long trip through wide fields, and past old rock formations. When we arrived I noticed a lot of cars there but I couldn't see any roads that led cross country which would have provided the cars access to the area. I assumed these people had come to see the Buddhist rock drawings as well but when we arrived at the site we were alone there.

The canyon walls through which the Ili River flows are quite steep. We were standing in the valley between two rock walls that towered overhead. I looked up from the valley to see if anyone was climbing the rock walls of the canyon. On one side, very high up, I see a group of people gathered under a rocky ledge. There is a woman sitting there, dressed in white, and she appears to be preaching to these people who are listening intently. I can't hear what she is saying as she is too far away.

Of course I am curious about what is going on and I ask the group from the Embassy if they want to go with me up to the rock to see what was happening. They say no as they are afraid, but my parents and I decide to find our way up the rock to where the woman is seated. As we got closer, I asked a few of the people who had been listening to the woman speak what they were doing there. They did not want to tell me. Then I noticed that some of the people were slowly entering a cave carved deep into the rocks.

We went to the woman in white and I asked her if we could go into the cave. At first she was very reluctant and then after a few moments she gave us permission to enter the cave. Another woman dressed in white was sitting in front of the cave as we walked by. Inside the cave the rocks were very white but the cave walls were black. I didn't know if the cave had been painted black or was naturally black, but it was very impressive. There were no lights in the cave but there were candles everywhere. It was very beautiful. A passageway led out of the cave and took people to a higher level to the top of a rock formation.

I followed the crowd of people and saw a man standing with arms outstretched, eyes closed, facing the sun. I kept asking people what was going on, but no one wanted to talk to us. The woman who had been seated in front of the cave was very angry we were there, so we left. I later discovered that the people we saw were worshippers of the Sky God Tengri and the Goddess Eje, who is the Goddess of the earth and moon. Eje in Mongolian literally translated to "mother" and is a variation of the Turkish Goddess Umay, the Goddess of fertility.

Accidentally witnessing this ancient pagan ritual, performed in modern day Kazakhstan, started me thinking about paganism.

I started to notice things I hadn't seen before – like ribbons tied to trees in the countryside. I learned through my research that many people in Kazakhstan are still pagan – especially the common people. During the years in which Kazakhstan was governed by Russia, there was never an emphasis placed on educating the people in the manner that Europeans and Americans were educated. The Soviets believed that if people remained ignorant they were easier to rule.

I had considered myself an atheist up until this point in my life. I knew that others worshipped Gods outside of Muslim or Christianity, but never saw this until now. It was a very moving experience. When I returned to Poland, I kept on thinking about it and thought it would be an interesting research project to see if these kind of pagan practices existed elsewhere in Europe. It was Halloween and of course I didn't know it was one of the pagan holidays. I started Googling key words like pagan, neo pagan, witchcraft, and then Wicca. From the very first moment I started reading about Wicca, I knew it was the religion for me. Up until this time, I never had any kind of mystic experience. I wouldn't even call the experience while in Kazakhstan mystical – it was just something interesting

I saw. I never had a vision, or a premonition.

But I knew beyond any doubt that traditional Wicca was what I wanted to learn. I also discovered immediately that there were no witches in Poland. I was not interested in learning alone, or teaching myself Wicca. I knew I had to find a Coven in which I could learn properly. Then I saw a photograph of Maxine Sanders. I decided that I wanted to be with people like her. I spent the next few years reading as much as I could about Wicca. I joined some public internet forums through which I was able to communicate with other pagans but nothing felt right to me. It would be another three years before my Initiation into the Craft.

I was born in Lodz, Poland. It is a huge town, the second largest city in Poland. Many pagans tell me they were born in the country or had a connection to nature as a child. This was not my reality. I was born into an urban environment. I wasn't connected with nature in childhood. My family lived a very cosmopolitan lifestyle and I spent a lot of time studying. I was very much into classical and Nordic mythology. I drew pictures of Olympian and Norse Gods but never thought of worshipping them. I never visited the forest or country. My parents worked all the time. I was in school and had a lot of classes. Unlike most children, I never had a pet. I did not have time to take care of one.

My parents were good people. They loved me very much. My father is a freethinker and an atheist. My mother considered herself Christian, but she was a true Witch at heart.

In my family there were lots and lots of very strong women. None considered themselves a witch but there were certain things about them which were very interesting from a Wiccan point of view. For example, as a kid I was into Norse mythology and bought myself a set of runes. My interest in the runes was not as a religious tool, but a general interest in mythology. My grandmother found the runes and took them away. She told me that they actually work and are not for kids. She said I was too young to use them.

This was strange because she was the most devout Christian in our family. Obviously she didn't think the runes were mumbo jumbo or devilish. She just said I was too young to read them. This was kind of strange to me. She once told me her parents organized spiritual séances where they invoked ghosts – this was not typical of what a Polish family would do because we are a very Catholic country. A few years ago I asked my grandmother if the stories she told were meant to scare me. She said she would never want to scare me, but that she wanted to make me aware of other worlds. She said it was important for me to act responsibly when working with the occult.

My mother kept on saying she didn't think that God is like the Church describes him. She even said that she doesn't think he is actually male – not that she thought he was female – but that she didn't think he was male in the way that the Church said he was. She said God was really connected to Nature in the same way that the women in my family were connected. They knew how to work with herbs, for example, which is something I never learned until after my Initiation.

My mother was very strong willed, especially when talking about heaven. She said that heaven was a place where you meet people you loved during your life. She had lots of interesting ideas that weren't openly pagan or had anything to do with witchcraft She knew a lot of things instinctively.

Since she died, I sometimes recall lots and lots of these things. When I meet her friends and the people she knew when she was young, they tell me stories about her and I get to know her again from their perspective. I find many of these experiences to be very close to what I am experiencing both inside and outside the Circle. Her way of thinking and reacting to the world around her is similar to the way I think as a Witch.

My Initiation into Alexandrian Witchcraft took place in April 2007 in London, England.

I'm a very intellectual type of guy. Since that first awakening of interest in Wicca following my trip to Kazakhstan, I read enormous numbers of books. I wanted to see how Covens worked, what witches think, and to understand the history of witchcraft. I was also trying to connect with Nature. Saying I was not a country boy before is an understatement. I met a few people who had been in touch with Covens, but when I got to know them I wasn't sure I wanted to belong to them. I spent about three years intensely studying witchcraft and searching for a Coven that was right for me.

Then I connected with the Temple of Stella Maris in South London. Scott, the High Priest of the Temple, had placed an ad on Witchvox. I decided to write to him and he asked me to call him. When we started to talk and I found out the Temple name, everything started to click. I was sure this was the Coven I was searching for. I wanted to travel to London to meet him, although it was not easy for me to organize everything. My life was filled with very tough moments at the time. My mother was ill with cancer, and I had constant problems at work. But despite all of this I knew

I had found the right people.

I went to London not knowing anyone. I had never been to England before this. It seemed like a completely insane thing to do. Now I understand it was one huge step of faith.

When I make up my mind to do something, it is no longer a problem. I didn't focus on the fact that this was a new city and that I was going to see people I had never met who were witches. I just believed that this was the right thing for me to do. I knew in my heart that things would work out. The trip was very easy and went smoothly. I knew there was a chance I would not be accepted. I was told if I wasn't accepted, I would have to wait another year before asking again. If I wasn't accepted the second time, I would have to wait another year. I knew before that first meeting that this was where I belonged. And that if it took one year or two years or three years, I would wait.

A few weeks after the first meeting I was accepted.

It was a challenge training long distance. I tried to get to London once a month – once every few months at a minimum. It was always tough for me. I had lots of work to do in Poland and was caring for my mother. Scott gave me things to do on my own, but being an Alexandrian witch to me means working in a group. You can't do proper ritual by yourself. There were moments when I was depressed to be so far from my own Coven, but the weak points in my training only made me stronger because I was less dependent on the Coven and had to get by on my own. It was an effort for me, but I wanted to make 200% of everything that I did. For me, witchcraft is always very intense. None of my rituals were wasted. The time spent inside the Circle triggered lots of experiences outside the Circle. Everything was in tune with the magic worked by the Coven.

Obviously it would be nice to have a Coven just around the corner, in the same city, or even in the same country. But working with the Temple of Stella Maris in London helped me to grow more quickly and learn more effectively. The magical work I was doing was intense on so many levels. I believe that the work of a witch, done within the Circle, should be taken outside the Circle. The rituals we do are only the base of our work. Our lives take us into contact with non-initiates and we can do the work of the Priesthood in many situations. I realized this quickly because I wasn't in Circle very often and was able to observe more of what was happening on the outside.

For me being a Priest is about service to my Gods. This is the most important thing for me. Other things that mean a lot to me are healing and teaching. As a Priest, I am obliged to bring other Initiates into the Craft. I feel that there are many Old Souls being reborn these days. They were Witches before and now they are searching for their way back to the Craft. I want to help them find their way back, as my Coven has helped me.

I have a partner who is also Craft. He is four years younger than me. It was our interest in the Craft that brought us together. When I first made contact with the Polish pagan community, I met him and we started to talk. We met at Yule and were a couple by Candlemas. He is a gift from the Gods. He will be taking his Initiation into the Alexandrian tradition in the very near future and I will no longer have to travel to London alone.

Our Coven works a lot with healing energy, which is very important to me. I often act as a healer in my own life. This is very much connected with my work as a Priest. I don't have much experience in teaching but find that in the Polish pagan community now, people come to me with questions. My work with them is not formal, such as in a Circle. I try to offer advice when asked and to help in whatever way I can. I am now living in Warsaw. My long term goal is to lead a Coven in Poland.

I feel that my calling in life is to be a teacher. Lots of people who are not aware that I am a witch tell me this. A few weeks ago I met a girl who works with animal spirits. She has the ability to discover your animal spirit. When she was calling those spirits for me, she said there was a dog and a wolf among them. She told me that the dog is a symbol of a teacher and that is what I would do soon. I also understand that the dog is a symbol of Hecate, who is a Goddess very important to me.

I sometimes look back on my journey. When I first learned about the Craft there were no Witches in Poland. It didn't stop me from searching for Initiation and finally finding the Coven I belonged to. My way to Initiation wasn't easy. But all the difficulties didn't stop me. To the contrary, they only strengthened me. After my Initiation many things become even harder for me, but they only made my Craft richer.

The worst, saddest thing that happened to me was the slow and painful death of my mother. Yet even this became the foundation of my spiritual rebirth. I know that I will never quit. All my efforts move me forward. I believe in myself, I trust myself. And I believe and trust the power of my own commitment. That is what it means to me to be an Alexandrian Priest.

Nothing is really easy but everything that happens to us - even the difficult things makes us stronger. There will always be obstacles and problems. In many ways on very mundane levels, things were never easy for me. After my Initiation I was in a serious accident which resulted in many health problems. But believe it or not, this only made me appreciate the good moments all the more. When I think how much energy, how much money, and how many struggles it took to bring me to each Circle, I really appreciate each second of the time I am there.

All the difficulties we encounter in our lives are a test. Life does not become easy because you say you want to develop spiritually or find your place in the universe. We each need to accept that and take an active part not in just our own life but in the life of our community, however we see community. We can't do this without facing problems. We have to face these problems and solve the ones we can. We also need to realize that there are some problems that can't be solved. Sometimes you just have to let them be.

This all strengthens you and enriches your Craft. It changes you on every possible level as a Priest, as a Witch, and as a human being.

I look at most of the problems I encounter as a gift. They could break me but I was never afraid to face them. And in facing them I am able to use all the skills I learned in the Circle. For me, the Circle is never an empty ritual, saying beautiful phrases, and waving my athame. I know I am learning within the Circle the lessons I will need outside the Circle. Without the challenges in life, I would never know how much I learned. My Craft would be very shallow.

There was a point after my Initiation when I realized that we have to live our Craft constantly. We have to face these difficulties and go where others are afraid to go. We have to face the darkness and this is a challenge to us. The core of our rituals requires us to meet death face to face. We do not run away, nor are we paralyzed by fear.

When we make mistakes, we learn from them. Then we are able to share those mistakes with others so they can learn with us. We all learn and grow together. Our mistakes become as much a part of our tradition as our success. We inherit both the problem and the solution.

# The Garden of Possible Things

*Meagan*
**Third Degree High Priestess**
**United States of America**

*The tractor moves through the field in a grumbling way. It is Autumn and the first frost, yet to be realized, stirs in the air like a promise long forgotten. As she and the other volunteers work hard to bring in a delicate crop, Meagan smiles. She knows the secrets of the harvest. She understands the cycle of life and death and rebirth better than most who work on the farm. Give to the earth and she won't fail, she thinks aloud. She whispers a thank you to the Old Gods for a bountiful harvest – a bounty that will be shared in homes where money is scarce and children know the pain of going to bed without supper.*

There was something odd about my roommate's boyfriend. Not odd in a bad way, he was just different.

The year was 1984 and my roommate started dating a man who said he was a witch. He was part of a large Boston based Coven and would talk with us about magic and witchcraft. I went to several open rituals and to a large pagan gathering called *Rites of Spring*. It was during this time that I realized that other people had the same experiences as me and I felt I had found a place to belong. I did not consider myself a witch at that point, but rather a neo-pagan. After a friend and I created a spell to find new and better apartments, I began to think I might have the makings of a Witch.

I was born in Southwestern Pennsylvania. My father was first generation; a son of Italian immigrants. He was a Roman Catholic, but did not go to church much when we were growing up. He was a printer and graduated from high school after the fall of the stock market in 1929. He liked the outdoors and hunted and fished. He took us kids fishing and hiking. He died in 2000 at the age of 87.

My mother was of Scottish, English and German ancestry and in many ways I have always seen her as a study in contradictions. She was a gifted Tarot reader, but did not believe in the Occult. She was an agnostic but made sure her children went to Sunday school. She was a heavy smoker and died from emphysema in 1990.

Both my parents lived during the Great Depression and the Second World War. They were both Aries and both were stubborn. I have two brothers: one two years older, the other five years younger.

When I was a child we lived in a rural area in Westmoreland County, Pennsylvania. My parents did not allow us to have a television, so I was not inclined to sit for hours in the house. I wanted to go outside and play. I spent as much time as I could outdoors and in the woods. It was there that I first encountered nature spirits. The only person I ever told about this was my great-grandmother. My Grandma lived with us while

I was growing up. She was a good Presbyterian who just so happened to believe in fairies and nature spirits. She told me to be careful because not all fairies were nice. In particular she instilled a real fear in me of water spirits. It took me years to learn how to swim.

My parents were not outwardly religious. My father became more involved in the Catholic Church as he got older. My mother said she was agnostic. My younger brother converted to Judaism when he married, and he and his wife are raising their son in the Jewish faith.

Like many people in my generation, I used a spirit board with friends while I was in college. We did it as a fun thing at first, except that I began to realize that the connection we made during the sessions was real. While I had always been aware of the energy around me and from the earth, it was using the Ouija board that helped me begin to understand the connection between the two. My awareness of the earth's energy would be heightened after we would use the Ouija board. It actually scared me. I felt as if I was being bombarded from all sides. It was opening up some channels that I had previously shut down in Junior High School because I didn't want to be different. It was in Junior High that my psychic abilities first began to cause me problems. I knew things that I had no way of knowing. It got me into trouble with friends.

At 13, my reaction was to suppress. At 19 – 20, I knew that I had to deal with this. I took a Transcendental Meditation class and began meditating. Meditation helped me focus and get a grip on all the stuff bouncing around me. I also stopped doing drugs on a regular basis at this time. Being stoned was too much input. During my 20s and early 30s I spent time in ashrams and at meditation retreats.

At 19 I was no stranger to the occult, my mother read Tarot cards. She picked up a deck in a second hand bookstore along with a couple of books when I was 16. By the time I was in college she was quite good at doing readings. I have a number of friends who used to want to go home with me so she could read their cards. It was only after looking at my own experiences that I began to realize that I too had some of my mother's abilities.

I went with my roommate and her boyfriend to hear Starhawk talk and participate in a full moon Circle at the Unitarian Universalist Church in Cambridge, Massachusetts in July 1984. I had been to a few new age type things before and to one very odd ritual when I was in college, but the full moon ritual with Starhawk was the first time I could feel the presence of a Goddess in Circle.

Throughout the 80s, I continued to read as much as I could and talked with other people about witchcraft. At that point I was not ready to join a traditional Coven. I needed to do some exploring on my own. I participated in public Sabbats whenever possible and for a short while Circled with a group of women who used Starhawk and Marion Weinstein's books as the basis of their rituals. They were nice women but only honored Goddesses, not Gods and I wanted both.

I spent some time in CUUPS (Covenant of Unitarian Universalist Pagan) Circles and went to some open circles in Salem run by students of Laurie Cabot. All of these experiences were OK, but not the right fit for me. In early 1993 I decided I wanted something more formal and traditional in the way of training and talked with a friend. We went together to a monthly Pagan/Wiccan coffee at a store in Marlborough, Mass. It was there that I met my teacher, Lady Morven, and several of her students. (One of those students later became my husband.) I applied for admission to the Coven and began studying with Lady Morven shortly thereafter. I was initiated into Alexandrian Craft in October 1993 by Lord Wolf's Head.

Being a Priestess for me is a way of life. If I am to honor and serve the old Gods then it must be manifest in how I live my life. As part of this, I worship the Gods, celebrate the wheel of the year, and open myself up to the energies of the earth, sun and moon. I also give freely of my time and energy to others. For me this has led me down a number of different paths.

On the magical level there are a few things in particular I can point to. I was the co-editor of a Neo-Pagan/Wiccan newsletter called *The Horns and Crescent*, which published for seven years from Samhain 1994 to Samhain 2001. I am also one of the founders of a Neo-Pagan church called *The Society of Elder Faiths* that holds public Sabbats and offers classes on various topics to our members.

I was also the High Priestess of an Alexandrian Coven for several years and, along with the other elders in the Coven, taught many students.

On the mundane level (although I do not consider this work mundane) I became involved with my local land trust, working to preserve open space here in Massachusetts and to promote the understanding of the importance of nature in the lives of all. I served on the board for nine years and left only when I served the maximum number of years allowed for a board member.

I also am very involved in hunger relief. I volunteer for an organization that runs a farm. At the farm we grow vegetables that are distributed throughout central Massachusetts by the local food bank. I do office work all year round and work with other volunteers during the growing season.

I see Alex Sanders as a complex human being. He was obviously a gifted magician and Witch. From everything I have read he was a good teacher, but not always very discriminating in his choice of students. I know some people were upset with his courting of the media during the '60s, but I think it fit the times. I do think that he could go overboard in the showmanship area. I also have a great deal of respect for him, because he persevered in his quest to have Witchcraft, the occult and magic seen as legitimate.

There is a lot of discussion lately about how important it is for the Craft to go on. I believe the Craft will always continue. Some people are drawn to traditional Covens and others to more eclectic paths.

There is also a lot of talk about how important it is to keep moving forward and not look back. Statements like this drive me crazy. There are times when such sentiments fit the work I am doing. Other times, I know that the blocks in my way are to be examined and learned from. I have learned over my lifetime that examining my course and questioning my motives is the right thing to do. I believe that just going forward without looking back and looking at motives and reactions is being blind to my own faults.

*Meagan parks the tractor next to the barn and shuts off the engine. There is a reluctant sputter and then silence. It has been a good day. Today's harvest is inside and will soon be on its way to the food bank. Her work on the farm is not easy. But like the other volunteers she knows that her efforts can make all the difference in the world to those in need.*

*Where once was a wall is now a door – a door that opens up not into want but into the garden of possible things.*

# The Open Door

*Karagan*
**Third Degree High Priest**
**United States of America**

*M*y story starts in 1997. I am a professionally trained actor and director. I was doing a play in Lisbon, Portugal which was nearing the end of its run. An actor's life may seem glamorous from the perspective of the audience but we don't have the benefit of always knowing where our next paycheck is coming from. I was struggling financially and worried about how I was going to pay the rent when this job ended.

One day I was talking with a fellow actor in the play, a friend named Patricia. She said I could light a candle and ask for money. Seeing that I was confused by her unexpected advice, she explained that this was a technique that was used in a religion called Paganism. She told me this was a spell that I could use to turn things around. I had heard about spells in books and movies but never imagined that people could do them in modern times. But I decided to give it a try. This experience taught me one of the first and most important occult lessons I would ever learn – that magic only works with passion. Without that intensity, everything that you do is an empty gesture.

The spell called for two ingredients – a candle and some anointing oil. The only candle I had was the candle I used whenever the power went off. It had been lit and re-lit a hundred times. Desperately I searched the apartment for oil – the only thing I could find was some scented baby oil in the bathroom. This is what I used to anoint and empower the candle, exactly as Patricia instructed.

A few days after doing the spell, the same director I was working with decided to do another play and he cast me before the current production ended. This play was even more successful than the previous one and I was able to continue to support myself for many months afterward.

From this point on I wanted to know more about magic and how it worked. Patricia directed me to a bookstore in the neighborhood where I lived that sold books on paganism and witchcraft.

I was absolutely disconnected from any religion at this time in my life. I always believed that there was some kind of power out there but refused to glue myself to the image of the old bearded man who was the God of the Christians. I didn't like what I had read about him. He was not the God of love but a God of vengeance and cruelty. He could be dangerous at times. I didn't know how these people could put out this propaganda that he was the God of mercy when this was obviously not true.

So one day I took Patricia's advice and went in search of this mysterious bookstore named Aquariana. I was surprised to realize I had passed this street many times and never noticed the store until now -

perhaps because from the outside the store appeared to be just a place that sold herbs for therapeutic use. But once inside there was a lot of Wiccan paraphernalia. I was surprised to see that the store carried books in English, which was very rare in Portugal at that time.

I was greeted by a gentle and kind woman named Isobel. Later I would discover that she was a Gardnerian High Priestess. She asked me how she could help me and I told her that I wanted every single book she had on Wicca. She laughed and said "Well, you'll have to take the whole shelf", and pointed to a long row of books on magic and witchcraft. I asked her to recommend a few books for me to get started with and she suggested I read *The Rebirth of Witchcraft* by Doreen Valiente, *To Stir a Magic Cauldron* by Silver Ravenwolf, and Raymond Buckland's *Complete Book of Witchcraft*. I read them avidly and immediately knew that Wicca was right for me. Isobel and her husband were organizers of the Portuguese chapter of Pagan Federation International. I began to get involved with PFI Portugal, participating in workshops and rituals. At the same time I continued to research the Craft to better understand what was going on in the world of witchcraft today.

Because the first book I read was by Doreen Valiente, I started my research with reading about Gardnerian Wicca. I read both of Gerald Gardner's books and learned of his account of the Old Religion. The feeling I got from Gardnerian Craft was that I was in the right place but with the wrong people. This wasn't my family.

Then one day while surfing the internet I learned of another branch of British Traditional Witchcraft called Alexandrian. This led me to read *The Witches Bible* by Stewart and Janet Farrar. This was where I wanted to be. I felt an immediate connection to Alexandrian Craft. The rituals were beautiful and moving. Looking back on the book now, I realize that these rituals were not purely Alexandrian as I know it today, but at the time I knew beyond any doubt that I wanted to be an Alexandrian. I wanted to know where this all came from. I knew the Farrars couldn't have made this all up.

Further research brought me to Alex Sanders. Alex fascinated me. I was captivated not only by him, but the vision of what he wanted the Craft to be. He had the same passion that I did. The same intensity that drove me to do that first spell, a spell born out of necessity and pushed forward by intent. A spell that I always knew would work because I believed with all my being that it would work. The Craft that Alex spoke of was not stagnant – there was movement there. It was going forward and I wanted to be a part of this.

I continued to work with Patricia for many months. I remember that we did our first Circle together. We used a book as a guide, but every detail of the Circle was personally attended to by me. I wanted it to be perfect. I remember it was such a solemn ritual – we knew it was a very serious thing and worked from the heart. I was concentrating so much on what was going on that I was trembling. Each word, each gesture, was powerful and fabulous and amazing. I had no doubt that what we were doing held great power.

I don't know who thought of it first, but one day she and I decided we wanted to dedicate ourselves to the Old Gods. She had studied for a while in Evora, a very old city in the south of Portugal. There is an ancient Cromlech there called Almendres. The stone megaliths that comprise the Circle date back to the Neolithic period.

It is a haunted place – echoing with the magic of centuries gone by and yet still as alive and vital today as when pagan worshippers first set foot in the ring of giant stones.

It was here that we decided to take our oaths before the Old Gods. She had a friend who agreed to drive us there late at night. Almendres is an active archeological and historic site so we had to be cautious not to be discovered. We prepared everything in advance. We made white robes and were naked beneath them. We arrived at the site in a thick mist – it was very cold and a bright full moon hung overhead. The ground was wet on our bare feet and the wind went right through the white robes. But we didn't care – every second of that experience is burned into my memory forever.

It would be years before I took my Initiation into Alexandrian Craft but this night was special – this was the moment in my life when I decided to follow the most ancient vocation of all. Under a Portuguese moon I gave my heart to the Gods and the Gods answered me back – I knew in my heart that I was their Priest.

I worked and studied in Portugal for another decade, always faithful to the Gods and always believing that when the time was right I would meet other Alexandrians and be welcomed home. It amazes me when people open themselves up to change and say to the Gods I will go anywhere and do anything that you want me to do – I will follow my path wherever it leads – and then expect to never travel outside the bounds of their city or country. My search for home took me to America. This is something I could have never imagined. I knew there were Alexandrians in the UK but at the time I hadn't connected with any of them.

For many reasons I was in touch with American witches and I was invited to visit Boston MA where there is a healthy population of Alexandrian Covens. This was the first line of Alexandrians that came to New England from London. I stayed in America for several months and was trained and initiated by this Coven before returning to Portugal. My heart was in the US and I returned again a few months later to continue my Craft education. After many more months of study and hard work I was initiated into second and third degree Alexandrian.

My first Initiation was the most significant experience of my life. The first Initiation renews you. When you are waiting to be initiated, you are flashing back to every single step that brought you to that point. It is a profound moment – a new awakening and at the same time a remembering of something familiar.

When I think about my role as a High Priest, I remember that Wicca is a Mystery tradition and that the most important work will always be within the Coven, working the Inner Mysteries of the temple. But I also believe it is important for the work of Priests and Priestesses of the Craft to extend beyond the Coven into the community. This can be in the smallest ways like cleaning a park, or helping people with food. It is very important that we help others whenever we can.

Teaching is also important. But a good teacher never stops learning and it is often the student who teaches the most valuable lessons. I believe that every single student has something to teach us - some lesson we need before we can go forward. It isn't always about just initiating people – the Craft is larger than that.

There is a pre-conceived idea that people have that, just because they have titles and degrees or are initiated, that they are immediately imbued with wisdom and knowledge and are absolutely magical. What is worse is that often these people have authority and power over others. We are talking about human beings after all and human nature is always very strange. We each react to things differently and one of those things is power.

The degrees are symbolic of power but that doesn't equate to power over but awakening power within. The Initiation can trigger things in you that you don't expect. It is a key to a lock – your lock. The key can fit into the lock and maybe even turn but that doesn't mean it will open the door. Sometimes it will turn and turn and not open the door. This happens despite the fact that the Initiation was done. It is not up to the initiate whether or not the door opens. It is not up to the initiators. You can have the highest degree in whatever tradition and still the door is closed.

The Mystery is that the door only opens when you're ready. It doesn't matter if you thought you were ready or your teachers thought you were ready. It is something that happens beyond us. There are no rules that mark this process. You can have all the books and all the books of shadows and all the degrees of every magical system in the world and sometimes the door just doesn't open. Some people take Initiation in this lifetime and die with a closed door. And sometimes the door opens on the first try.

I was born in Lisbon in the time of dictatorship. My parents were artists and came from a family of artists, so everyone was open-minded.

The official church of Portugal is the Roman Catholic Church. I remember my father and mother were both very sensitive to spirits and energies. My mom is Catholic but always said she is her own pope. She never cares what the Priest has to say and practices her own way. My mom was always supportive of the fact that I felt no connection to Catholicism. When I told her I was a witch, she was respectful and also very curious. My father didn't care if I was a Buddhist or Opus Dei or a Witch, he couldn't care less what path I chose.

I was three years old when the revolution happened in Portugal. I was a child at the time. My mom and I were in the street going to my grandmother's house. We were in Rua do Carmo, which was very close to the location where the final moments of the revolution took place. A man was running towards us, yelling for my mother to get inside a house because there were tanks and soldiers in the streets. We could hear gunshots being fired a few blocks away. In the marketplace, courageous women took carnations from the flower stalls and marched up to the soldiers with their rifles drawn. The women put the flowers in the barrels of the guns and stood silently before the soldiers. It was a moment in Portuguese history that changed the country forever.

When I was very young, I had this thing about sheets. I would go to visit my grandmother and take the sheets from the bed into the back yard. I rolled myself up in the sheets in what I understand now as the style of a Greek or a Roman aristocrat. Then I would walk regally around the garden picking plants and flowers to make potions. My grandmother was disgusted by it and very unhappy with the bottles of green stuff I created. I still don't know what was happening but assume it was a past life memory of being an alchemist of some type.

Portugal was, and is, a land filled with folk magic. I remember when my father left my mother; she wanted to work magic to bring him back. She went to this man in the town who made potions and teas and sold them to people who needed his help. He sold my mother a bag of herbs for a lot of money and told her to make a tea and drink it every night. She was also instructed to take a bit of my father's underwear, light a candle, and read a prayer to the moon every night before an open window. She also had to take a kitchen knife and make some sort of sigils with the knife toward the moon.

I was a child at the time and we were living alone. She asked me to help her because it was difficult for her to hold the paper with the prayer and do everything else at the same time. So we're standing there in front of an open window and she was doing all of this stuff and reading the prayer to the moon. I laughed because I thought it was funny. She warned me first and then when I didn't stop she slapped me. She was afraid the spell wouldn't work and my father wouldn't come back because I was laughing. This was my earliest experience with Portuguese folk magic. Even today in Portugal there are these men and women who do spells and sell them to people.

When I think of Alex Sanders, I recognize that he was a phenomenal person who is a very rare example of an open door. He is an example of an extremely magical man. Many people compare him to Gerald Gardner but Gardner didn't have half of the magical ability Alex had. And that is not meant in disrespect to Gardner. People just have to realize it is true. Above all, Alex was certainly the King of his witches.

Alex was a very special man. Ultimately, he dared. And that's what sets him apart. He dared to go beyond what was given to him. He not only opened his own door, but many other doors will open because of him and Maxine.

The Alexandrian tradition today is going through a state of consciousness and a period of self-realization. People are starting to think about the tradition in new ways. There is a lot of passion now and the Alexandrian tradition is becoming aware of its own Corpus. We are talking to each other and learning from each other. We perceive each other's practices, and understand both the similarities and differences between us. Although we are the Hidden Children of the Goddess, we have to communicate with each other so we can evolve. This is what pushes us forward – this is the perpetual movement Alex talked about.

The important thing is to worship the Old Gods – it doesn't matter if it is just one candle lighting the dark, or one stick of incense. The very act of worshiping the Old Gods carries us forward. As long as the Temple lights are lit, we will survive.

# EPILOGUE

*It* is not uncommon for a writer to put his characters to bed, figuratively speaking, once a book is finished. So much time is spent in the creative process that when the time comes for them to walk and talk on their own the writer is only a little sad to turn them out into the universe.

But this is different. These characters are not fictional and they do not lie down easily. They stomp around my head at night and keep me awake. They refuse to be quiet and are not easily lost in a metaphor or a clever turn of a phrase.

These are real people and their stories are told proudly. I can't ignore them, nor would I want to. The tellers share more than words - they whisper profound things - both dark and beautiful. In their stories I see myself.

I am Lyn, knees scraped from climbing, up a tree and praying for daylight. I am Karagan under the cold Portuguese moon. I am Tanith, sad about losing the rabbit but happy about that last minute deal with God. I am Oskar who in a moment of heartbreak realizes that some problems cannot be solved. I am Dean swimming with sharks and Theitic on his way to Pluto.

I have never climbed a tree or buried a rabbit. But I have hoped and loved and believed with every fiber of my being that things would work out even when the odds were against me.

What connects us is not the moments that make up our lives but what's behind these moments. Alex is the thread that binds each of these stories together. He is the founder of the feast.

But there are other feasts and other tables. It is around these tables that new stories will be told.

So I raise a glass to Alex and say thank you. How could you have ever known what you started?

I also drink to you, dear reader. When the time comes to tell your story, tell it loudly. Don't hold back. Stomp and yell and make them hear you.

Every word you speak is magic. And magic brings change. Together with every other teller you weave a magnificent spell - a spell that makes all stories one story.

If you enjoyed *All the King's Children*, you will also enjoy *A Voice in the Forest, Spirit Conversations with Alex Sanders*. This classic of pagan literature is now in its last US printing - limited quantities remain.

Get your copy at **www.logiosprojects.com**

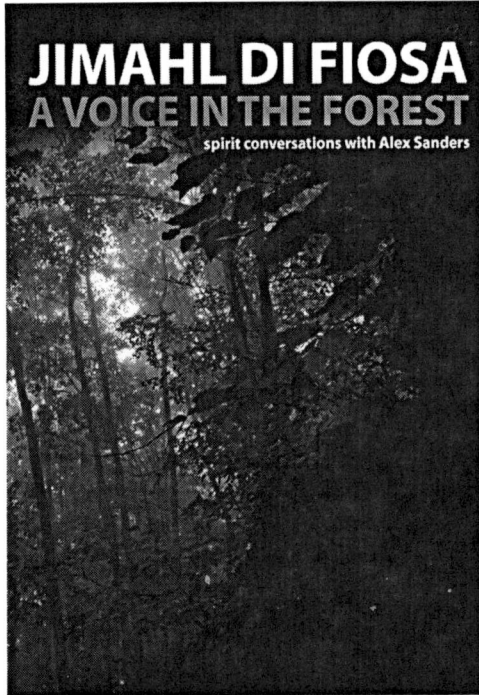

Fully ten years after the death of Alex Sanders, a handful of witches began experimenting with a spirit board. An entity responded and identified iself as Alex and proceeded to prove that claim.

What readers are saying about *A Voice in the Forest*

*"A true classic!"*
*"Extraordinary!"*
*"Impossible to put down"*
*"A true journey that will take you into the depths of magic, the Otherworld and what life beyond death can teach you".*

Lightning Source UK Ltd.
Milton Keynes UK
UKOW03f1845220517

301781UK00001B/220/P